Business Unit & Divisional Performance Measurement

Business Unit & Divisional Performance Measurement

MAHMOUD EZZAMEL

Price Waterhouse Professor of Accounting and Finance
The Manchester School of Management
The University of Manchester Institute of Science and Technology

$$C \mid I \mid m \mid A$$

Published in association with The Chartered Institute of
Management Accountants

ACADEMIC PRESS

Harcourt Brace Jovanovich, Publishers
London   San Diego   New York
Boston   Sydney   Tokyo   Toronto

This book is printed on acid-free paper

ACADEMIC PRESS LIMITED
24–28 Oval Road
LONDON NW1 7DX

United States Edition published by
ACADEMIC PRESS INC.
San Diego, CA92101

A catalogue
record for this
book is available
from the British
Library

ISBN
0–12–245670–X

Typeset by Photo·graphics
Printed in Great Britain by
Mackays of Chatham plc,
Chatham, Kent

Contents

Series Editor's Preface

David Otley
KPMG Peat Marwick Professor of Accounting
Lancaster University

A major problem for the management accounting teacher has been the selection of a suitable text for advanced courses. Although a number of very good texts exist, they typically do not include some topics that individual teachers wish to teach. On the other hand, they do include a considerable amount of material on topics that are unnecessary for a particular course. Students often feel that they have a poor deal in purchasing large and expensive texts that do not cover the whole of their course, yet include large amounts of extraneous material.

This series is an attempt to resolve this problem. It will consist of a set of slim volumes, each of which deals with a single topic in depth. A coherent course of study may therefore be built up by selecting just those topics which an individual course requires, so that the student has a tailor-made text for the precise course that is being taken. The texts are aimed primarily at final year undergraduate courses in accounting and finance, although many will be suitable for MBA and other postgraduate programmes. A typical final year advanced management accounting option course could be built around four or five texts, as each has been designed to incorporate material that would be taught over a period of a few weeks. Alternatively, the texts can be used to supplement a larger and more general textbook.

Each text is a free-standing treatment of a specific topic by an authoritative author. They can be used quite independently of each other, although it is assumed that an introductory or intermediate-level management accounting course has been previously taken. However, considerable care has been taken in the choice and specification of topics, to ensure that the texts mesh together without unnecessary overlap. It is therefore hoped that the series will provide a valuable resource for management accounting teachers, enabling them to design courses that meet precise needs whilst still being able to recommend required texts at an affordable price.

For the memory of Kenneth Hilton

Introduction

The pervasiveness, and persistence, of multidivisional organisations in modern Western and North American economies has been one of the most notable business phenomena of the modern era. Pioneered in the 1920s by the giant General Motors, this organisational innovation was diffused widely both inside and outside the USA, to become the most dominant organisational form. The meteoric rise and persistent dominance of the multidivisional organisation gave rise to numerous fundamental questions: Are multidivisional organisations more profitable than organisations employing alternative organisational forms? What are the attributes which are so specific to the multidivisional form? What are the best means by which corporate funds can be allocated among competing divisions? What are the optimum levels of decision-making autonomy which should be permitted to divisional managers by top management? How are divisional managers best motivated to operate in a manner which is consistent with the overall interest of the whole organisation? How can top management sensibly evaluate the performance of each division and also of their managers? What types of information are needed to guide divisional managers in making day-to-day decisions? And how can such information be generated?

Many similar questions have also been asked, relating for example to issues such as optimal transfer pricing and reward schemes, but these are outside the scope of this book. The important point, however, is that the above questions raise issues which are central to the design of accounting systems in divisionalised organisations and to the manner in which such systems are used.

Numerous writers have devoted much of their attention to addressing the above questions. Many of these contributions were published in scholarly journals, and these are examined in some detail here. In addition, three specialist books have also been published: David Solomons' *Divisional Performance: Measurement*

1

and Control (Financial Executives Research Foundation, 1965), Cyril Tomkins' *Financial Planning in Divisionalised Companies* (Haymarket, 1973), and Richard Vancil's *Decentralization: Ambiguity by Design* (Irwin, 1979). Collectively, these three books have contributed significantly to the advancement of our knowledge in this field.

Although the above three books should be viewed as complementary to this volume, there are three main differences which merit noting. First, of necessity the present volume deals with only a sub-set of the topics discussed in these books: namely performance evaluation of divisions and business units. Other topics, such as transfer pricing and reward systems, are dealt with in separate volumes in this series. Second, it has been possible to examine some of the important recent literature which was not available to earlier authors. This volume therefore offers an up-to-date, state of the art review of the relevant literature. Third, and most important, the performance evaluation issue is approached not only from an economic perspective, which is the dominant approach most notably in the Solomons and Tomkins books, but also from the broader organisation theory perspective. Hence, among other things this volume examines the role of structural controls, such as divisional environment, divisional interdependence, divisional size, managerial autonomy, internal audit systems and so on, in the context of performance evaluation. Similarly, some space is devoted to a discussion of the relevance of non-financial, but quantitative information as well as qualitative information relevant to the appraisal of divisional performance.

Despite these differences it should be noted that this volume focuses on providing a *technical*, rather than radical, overview of the literature. Many of the arguments presented here draw on ideas developed in my book *Advanced Management Accounting: An Organisational Emphasis*, written with Barney Hart (Cassell, 1987). Nevertheless, numerous other arguments were developed specifically for the present volume. My intended audience includes primarily final-year undergraduates and postgraduate students taking advanced courses in management accounting, but I also hope that the book will be relevant to managers and academics at large.

I would like to acknowledge my indebtedness to many colleagues and friends for stimulating my interest in studying the theory and practice of divisional accounting systems. Having barely been introduced to this topic as a PhD student at Asyut University, Egypt, under the guidance of Professor Mustafa Abdel-Motaal, I had to abandon the project six months later to take up a PhD scholarship at the University of Southampton. During that period, and for many years later, I benefited significantly from the advice of Dr Barney Hart and Mr Desmond McComb. My PhD thesis was supervised by the late Professor Kenneth Hilton and it was due to his constant encouragement and his continuous invaluable intellectual stimulation that I managed to successfully complete my thesis. He was extremely generous with suggestions and advice as well as with his time. My intellectual indebtedness to him is enormous.

I also owe a special debt to Professor David Otley, for it was he in the first instance who approached me about writing this volume. David read the manuscript very thoroughly and made numerous helpful comments which have undoubtedly improved the text.

My thanks to Lizzie Burrows who worked patiently and speedily on word processing the manuscript.

My wife, Ann and my children Adam, Nadia and Samia suffered the trials and the deprivations that are typically inflicted upon authors' families. Their patience and support has helped to maintain my enthusiasm.

Mahmoud Ezzamel
Manchester
July 1991

1

The Emergence and Attributes of Multidivisional Structures

The emergence of the multidivisional form has been one of the most far-reaching developments in the history of organisations. Indeed, Williamson (1970, p. 175) has characterised this structural form as "American capitalism's most important single innovation of the 20th Century". Once invented, it quickly became established as the dominant form of structuring, particularly in the business sector. This prevalent organisational form has several important implications for accounting, for it poses major questions as to how one can design suitable systems of performance evaluation, methods of pricing and allocating intra-organisational flows of goods and resources, schemes for rewarding managers, and finely-tuned combinations of financial and non-financial performance indicators. But before some of these important issues can be addressed here, it would be expedient to clarify some of the terminology we use and elaborate the virtues of the divisionalised form. Hence, this chapter starts by drawing the necessary distinctions between the interrelated concepts of centralisation, decentralisation and divisionalisation. This is followed by an exposition of the arguments for and against the divisionalised form, and then by an exploration of some of the evidence relating to its prevalence among organisations. There follows a discussion of the objectives of divisional performance measurement and definitions of major sub-units which can be the subject of accounting measurement. Finally, a brief summary brings together the salient points thus far discussed.

CENTRALISATION, DECENTRALISATION AND DIVISIONALISATION

Definitions

The concepts of centralisation, decentralisation and divisionalisation are interrelated, which partly accounts for their confused use at times by both academics and practitioners. The most common confusion relates to treating decentralisation and divisionalisation as synonymous, when, as will be demonstrated later the two terms differ significantly. According to Simon (1954, p. 1):

> An administrative organization is centralized to the extent that decisions are made at relatively high levels in the organization; decentralized to the extent that discretion and authority to make important decisions are delegated by top management to lower levels of executive authority.

The above definition indicates that the terms "centralisation" and "decentralisation" are relative, since absolute measures of either term are only likely to be used as theoretical constructs. But the definition begs the question of which decisions are important and which are not? Also, what does "relatively high levels in the organisation" mean? These ambiguities pose difficulties in distinguishing between the terms, as will be illustrated below. Decentralised structures can be either "functional" or "federal" (see Ezzamel and Hilton, 1980a). "Functional" decentralisation refers to the delegation of decision-making power to lower managerial levels on the basis of functional specialisation, for example production, marketing, etc. "Federal" decentralisation involves the partitioning of the firm into two or more quasi-autonomous sub-units (i.e. divisions or business units) whose activities are coordinated primarily through market and/or administrative price mechanisms, for example divisions dealing with different product lines, different customers, or different geographical areas. This implies that divisionalisation is a special case of, but not synonymous with, decentralisation. But even this distinction is incomplete, for it implies that *all* divisionalised firms are decentralised. Indeed, some divisionalised organisations are highly decentralised, with delegation of decision-making power permeating their structures. However, in some other divisionalised firms many important decisions are delegated to division managers, but with only limited discretion below that level (Mintzberg, 1979; Emmanuel, Otley and Merchant, 1990). Such firms will be characterised then as having delegated decision-making at the divisional management level, but with the divisions themselves being highly centralised and highly structured from within.

Some attributes of divisionalised firms

Examination of the attributes and characteristics of divisionalised firms has received the attention of many researchers, among whom Williamson has been one of the most prominent. Williamson (1970; 1975) developed a framework for the analysis of organisational form, distinguishing between centralised structures, or what he calls the unitary form (or U-form) and divisionalised structures, which he calls the multidivision form (or M-form). As we will see later, he makes the distinction between the two structures on the basis of their ability to minimise transactions cost.

According to Williamson, a major attribute of the M-form relates to the allocation of responsibility for differing decisions; strategic decisions are vested in top management, whereas operating decisions are the prerogative of divisional managers. This distinction is said to have major advantages as discussed later; more importantly, however, an additional crucial attribute is that the M-form evolves the requisite control apparatus needed for effective performance in a profit-maximising sense. This requisite control apparatus comprises three parts:

1. An incentive mechanism, utilising both pecuniary and non-pecuniary rewards, which can be manipulated to align the interests of divisional managers with those of top management.
2. An internal audit system which develops suitable measures of performance against which it reviews and evaluates the performance of divisional managers and of their divisions.
3. An allocation system which assigns cash flows to the most profitable alternatives as evaluated by top management, rather than allowing such resources to simply revert back to the divisions in which they originated.

Williamson further argued that to ensure the attainment of optimal divisionalisation, corporate structural designers must engage in:

1. The identification of divisional boundaries (which in turn relates to defining divisional environment and technology, determining divisional size and defining divisional interdependencies).
2. The assignment of a quasi-autonomous status to each division (determining the extent of divisional autonomy).
3. The allocation of company resources to divisions.
4. The use of performance measures and reward schemes to monitor divisional activities.
5. The performing of strategic planning whenever possible.

Clearly, firms will not always fall neatly into either the U-form or M-form categories. Hybrid, as well as other, structures are likely to emerge, depending upon the extent to which the attributes of the pure M-form are violated. Hence a more complete set of structural configurations will include the following (see Williamson and Bhargava, 1972):

Unitary (U-form): a traditional, functionally organised enterprise, including those with a degree of diversification which accounts for less than a third of the firm's value added.

Holding company (H-form): a divisionalised enterprise for which the requisite internal control apparatus has not been provided because of the subsidiary nature of divisions.

Multidivisional (M-form): a divisionalised enterprise in which a separation of operating from strategic decision-making is attained and for which the requisite internal control apparatus has been provided and is systematically employed.

Transitional multidivisional (M'-form): an M-form enterprise in the process of adjustment and learning.

Corrupted multidivisional (M̄-form): a divisionalised enterprise with the requisite control apparatus but .where the central management is extensively involved in operating activities.

Mixed (X-form): an enterprise in which H-form structure, M-form divisions, and even centrally supervised divisions, may exist simultaneously.

Whilst both the U-form and the M-form are deemed optimal structures under certain specific conditions, the remaining structures are considered non-optimal, as they fail to minimise transactions cost and hence reduce profitability to levels below those assumed to be generated under neoclassical economic models of the firm.

THE ARGUMENTS FOR AND AGAINST DIVISIONALISATION

Conventionally, arguments elaborating the case for and against divisionalisation tended to be considered paralleled to those relating to decentralisation. Subsequently, however, arguments more specific to divisionalisation have been developed (e.g. Williamson, 1975; Ezzamel and Hilton, 1980a; Spicer and Ballew, 1983; Ezzamel, 1985).

The arguments for divisionalisation

The arguments for divisionalisation are frequently rooted, either explicitly or implicitly, in the main thesis of contingency theory, according to which organisation structure should be carefully matched to situational contingencies. Chandler (1962), for example, argued that the M-form emerged in response to increased organisational complexity, which is caused not only by growth in firm size but also by greater diversification into new lines of business and increased vertical integration across widely separated geographical areas. Although large size creates problems related to sheer volume, these can be dealt with in centralised structures through the use of standard operating rules and procedures and increased reliance on administrative and support staff. Diversity, however, poses more daunting problems. As diversity increases, technical expertise becomes more localised, as in the case of geographical diversity, and hence it becomes difficult, may be even impossible, for central management to make informed decisions. In a divisionalised structure these problems can be dealt with efficiently, as central management need to focus only on strategic decisions whereas day-to-day operating decisions are delegated to lower managerial levels. Similarly, contingency theorists contend that as the firm increasingly operates in diverse markets, increases in size, grows older, employs divisible technologies, and becomes less dependent upon other organisations, so the optimal organisational structure becomes the M-form (see Ezzamel and Hart, 1987).

When the M-form is deemed the optimal structure, the organisation is said to reap the following benefits (see Williamson, 1975; Spicer and Ballew, 1983; Ezzamel, 1985):

Efficient allocation of resources

Compared to the external capital market, the M-form, through its internal mechanisms, can allocate resources more efficiently, because it can: (a) obtain required information at a low cost; (b) make fine-tuning (e.g. impose incremental monetary sanctions) as well as discrete adjustments (e.g. discontinue a division); and (c) monitor performance economically through the use of performance ratings, incentives and control mechanisms.

Efficient information transmission

By delegating much of the decision-making power to lower managerial levels, communication channels to higher levels need not be overloaded by information relevant only to lower levels. Further economies are achieved by grouping highly interacting activities *within* a single division, so as to minimise inter-divisional interactions.

Minimising sub-optimal behaviour

The M-form achieves this in a number of ways: (a) by vesting strategic decisions in top management and operating decisions in divisional management, problems caused by uncertainty/complexity are reduced because of specialised decision-making. In contrast, under the U-form operating managers can become too involved in strategic decisions, thus maximising the creation of slack and non-pecuniary benefits; (b) by focusing on cooperation between transacting parties the potential for opportunistic behaviour is reduced, in contrast to market-mediated transactions which engender selfish interest; (c) by employing an internal control mechanism to monitor performance continuously using sensitive performance ratings and a flexible reward structure; and (d) by breaking deadlocks in bargaining situations economically, as conflicts and disputes can be resolved by fiat.

The arguments against divisionalisation

The case for divisionalisation is not as straightforward as the above discussion appears to imply. For example, when markets are fairly efficient, they are unlikely to be inferior substitutes to internal organising through the M-form. Further, there are two arguments which can render divisionalisation a less efficient form of structure:

Excessive interdependence: This could arise when (a) the corporate objective function (main goal) is indivisible into divisional objective functions (divisional goals) without imposing significant externalities (i.e. interdependencies between divisional objectives); (b) if corporate resources are complementary, such that their segmentation among various divisions impairs the potential for economies of scale and scope; and (c) if divisional production functions are interdependent. The costs of managing these interdependencies effectively can be extremely high, and at the limit can exceed any benefits which may be obtained from divisionalisation.

Costs triggered by divisionalisation: Although divisionalised structures can considerably economise certain types of transactions cost, they can also trigger off others which might otherwise have been avoided. For example, diversification through divisionalisation tends to be relatively expensive (Moyer, 1970).

The advocates of divisionalisation will contend that these disadvantages will arise only if divisionalised structures *other* than the M-form are adopted, for example the mixed form or the corrupt form (see Williamson, 1975). However, it must be recognised that while so many firms are organised along the pure M-form, many others adopt the "less pure" forms, because many of the characteristics of the pure M-form cannot be easily maintained in practice. Hence, to the extent that divisionalised firms in the real world do not approximate the pure M-form, the proposed advantages of divisionalisation may not fully materialise.

Empirical evidence

Several empirical studies have been undertaken with the aim of testing the extent to which the divisionalised form outperforms other structural forms. Most of these studies have been stimulated by a hypothesis developed by Williamson (1970, p. 134), which came to be known as the M-form hypothesis:

> The organization and the operation of the large enterprise along the lines of the M-form favours goal pursuit and least-cost behaviour more nearly associated with the neoclassical profit maximisation hypothesis than does the U-form organizational alternative.

This hypothesis anticipates the benefits of the M-form discussed above, but these are now stated in terms of maximised profit as a result of minimised transactions cost. The results of most of the empirical studies yield support for the M-form hypothesis, but a number of studies are not supportive (for a review, see Ezzamel, 1985).

Those studies which are supportive of the M-form hypothesis were based on either American or British companies. Their main conclusions were: (a) while the M-form was being diffused there was a performance differential in favour of M-form firms compared with U-form firms in terms of earning superior rates of return on shareholders' equity (though by precisely how much differs across studies), and (b) once the divisional form became widespread, differential performance was not observed (as most firms have become "appropriately" structured).

The studies which provide no support for the M-form were conducted in Germany and Japan. Their main conclusion was that M-form firms showed a reduction in profitability for several years following the introduction of the M-form, with no evidence of any eventual positive gain. The results of the empirical studies are therefore not conclusive; this may be caused by:

1. Institutional and cultural differences between different countries. For example, in both Japan and Germany, banks play a much more central role in organising the flow of resources to firms, at levels which far exceed those observed in the USA and the UK.
2. Extraneous variables which may influence the observed results. Examples include the extent of ownership control and the extent to which effective control systems are employed to monitor agency costs.
3. Differences in corporate strategies between firms which may accord profitability different priorities in the short-run; this may be reflected in the results of these studies which were, in the main, conducted over short periods of time.

OBJECTIVES OF DIVISIONAL PERFORMANCE MEASUREMENT

Measures of divisional performance used in practice are typically financially focused, such as accounting profit, return on investment (ROI), residual income (RI) and sales revenue. In addition, frequent appeals have been made in the academic literature to broaden the choice of financial measures by incorporating measures such as discounted cash flows (DCF) and value added, and by buttressing financial measures in general with non-financial and qualitative measures, for example employee turnover and consumer satisfaction. An evaluation of these measures, however, begs the question: what are the aims that measures of performance are expected to serve in this context?

Traditionally, the literature indicates three main reasons for which an index of divisional profitability would be sought (see Solomons, 1965):

1. To guide central management in assessing the efficiency of each division as an economic entity, in order to facilitate making divisional viability decisions (e.g. whether to expand or reduce the activities of a particular division).

2. To help central management in assessing the efficiency with which divisional managers discharge their responsibilities in running their divisions. This need not be identical to (1) above, since some of the elements which impact upon the performance of a division may be beyond the control of its manager (for example, divisional share of Head Office expenses) and thereby should be excluded from the performance index of the latter.

3. To guide divisional managers in making decisions in respect of the daily activities of their own divisions. As will be demonstrated in subsequent chapters, the manner in which central management assesses the performance of divisional managers has a strong impact on the way managers make decisions.

Whilst these three objectives offer useful insights with respect to the underlying objectives of divisional performance measurement, they are narrowly conceived, because (a) they exclude internal uses of divisional performance measures below the divisional manager level, and (b) they focus only on internal uses, to the exclusion of external uses.

As regards the first omission, measures of divisional performance can be used by lower-level managers to monitor, or at least to influence, their divisional managers. For example, Williamson (1970) refers to pressure that can be exercised by lower-level participants on deviant divisional managers to bring them into line with corporate objectives, in order to prevent cuts in divisional resources which might be imposed by top management. This is because it is lower-level organisation members who are likely to be the most affected by reductions in divisional resources. Likewise, divisional financial results may be used by internal wage negotiators to assess corporate financial projections for collective bargaining purposes.

As regards the second omission, external users may include disaggregated divisional results into their assessments of the firm. For example, Ortman (1975) has reported that financial analysts who use disclosed segmental (divisional) data derive more accurate estimates of the per-share value of the firm's capital. Similar arguments can be made for assessing overall corporate riskiness and classifying a firm into the correct industrial group, and such data may be used not only by financial analysts, but also by existing investors, potential investors, bankers and other agencies. These needs underlie the increasing tendency towards companies' disclosure of financial information by major segments (divisions) in the USA, the UK and many EC countries.

RESPONSIBILITY CENTRES: SOME CLARIFICATIONS

In order to avoid ambiguity, we need at the outset to make some clarifying comments to distinguish different types of responsibility centre. A responsibility centre is a fairly general term which usually denotes the apportioning of responsibility (either collective or individual, but usually the latter) to a particular part of the organisation (for example a department, or a group of machines, or even one machine) or to some or one of its members (e.g. a single worker). The main characteristic here is that lines of responsibility can be traced down clearly from the manager in charge to the responsibility centre, and responsibility may be expressed in terms of costs and/or revenues, physical output, or quality of service.

This definition will help us in distinguishing between cost centres, profit centres, investment centres, revenue centres, and business units – all of which are responsibility centres. The only differences between them relate to the manner in which responsibility is expressed. Hence, in the case of a cost centre, responsibility relates to the monitoring of production/service flows and associated cost flows, whereas in the case of revenue centres concern is with the flow of revenues, without explicit attention to cost (because cost is likely to be either trivial or uncontrollable at that level). Further, in the case of profit centres responsibility relates to the flow of both costs and revenues, or simply to the maximisation of profit, where no account is taken of the level of investment in the centre. For an investment centre, responsibility does not simply relate to profitability in an absolute sense, but is related to the investment base of the centre, and thus performance tends to be measured in terms of profit as a percentage of investment levels (e.g. ROI).

Strategic business units (SBUs) reflect responsibility with respect to part of the organisation's strategic mission as it relates to specific areas of business activity. An example is the growth-share matrix developed by the Boston Consulting Group, which divides SBUs into *cash cows* (cash generators), *stars* (good prospects), *question marks* (uncertain profit potential) and *dogs* (candidates for divestment).

The design and use of performance evaluation mechanisms is largely dependent upon the type of responsibility centre being dealt with. For example, cost centres are usually monitored through the use of detailed cost standards and budgets, whereas profit centres can be monitored by means of summary profit statistics such as controllable profit or net profit figures. It is therefore imperative that the precise nature of the responsibility centre should be established clearly before a meaningful discussion of performance measures can take place.

SUMMARY

The purpose of this chapter has been to provide the necessary background for the remainder of this book. After clarifying the differences between the three interrelated concepts of centralisation, decentralisation and divisionalisation, we examined some of the basic attributes of divisionalised structures. We argued that while many divisionalised companies are highly decentralised, others have divisions which are highly centralised below the divisional management level. This was followed by an articulation of the arguments in support of, and those against, divisionalisation, and a brief summary of the results of empirical research which has sought to test for the existence of a performance differential in favour of divisionalised structures compared to other structures. We argued that much of the potential benefits of divisionalisation is unlikely to be fully recognised if structures other than the pure M-form emerge, and indeed the results of the empirical evidence are inconclusive as to whether divisionalisation is always the optimal structure. We then drew attention to the fact that while much of divisional performance results are used for the purposes of top-down internal monitoring, there is much scope, not only for its use internally by lower managers to influence higher managers and to shape collective bargaining agreements, but also for its use by a multitude of external users seeking to derive more accurate models of the firm, for example with respect to future performance. This was followed by a brief discussion of the differences between various types of responsibility centre, where we argued that the differences relate mainly to the way in which responsibility is expressed, for example cost flow, revenue flow, or profit flow. The adequacy of various performance measures in the context of divisionalised firms relies not only upon the objectives of performance measurement but also upon the precise type of flow to be monitored.

In the following chapter, we evaluate the suitability of traditional accounting measures of performance, referring in particular to the suitability of traditional accounting profit, return on investment, residual income and sales forecast.

QUESTIONS

1. Outline and explain the differences between the three concepts of centralisation, decentralisation and divisionalisation.
2. Identify some of the main attributes of the divisionalised structural form. Explore the extent to which these attributes are observable in organisations you are familiar with through (a) business history literature, and/or (b) direct access.
3. Discuss the arguments for and against the appropriateness of divisionalisation as a structural form. To what extent does the empirical evidence support these arguments?
4. Discuss and evaluate the objectives of divisional performance measurement. Comment on the extent to which you think the benefits of reporting on divisional performance exceed the costs of reporting.
5. Identify and distinguish different types of responsibility centre. Explore, giving examples, the extent to which different responsibility centres can be accommodated within a divisionalised company.

2

Traditional Accounting Measures of Performance

In the preceding chapter, the need was stressed for assessing the performance of sub-units, such as divisions and business units, and their managers. It was suggested that the choice of an appropriate performance index is partly dependent upon the precise type of responsibility centre under consideration, since some have responsibility for profit flows whereas others are responsible for the flows of both profit and capital. It was also pointed out that there is a multitude of users, both internal and external to the firm, who make use of divisional accounting information in various decision contexts.

An inspection of the literature indicates that measures of divisional performance developed so far divide broadly into two categories: traditional measures which are used widely in practice, and conceptually more appealing, but less widely applied measures. The traditional measures tend to be based on conventional accounting measurement techniques and they include accounting profit, return on investment (ROI), residual income (RI) and sales revenue. The less traditional measures focus primarily on the use of discounted cash flow (DCF).

In Chapter 1 it was stated that measures of divisional performance are useful to various users, both internal and external, in terms of assessing managerial, sub-unit, and corporate-wide performance. The multitude of uses to which measures of divisional performance can be put have stimulated a lively debate in the literature as to whether any single performance measure is sufficiently complete to satisfy the needs of different users, or whether *different* performance indices should be developed for different purposes. As will be indicated later in this chapter, the balance seems to be strongly in favour of the use of multiple performance measures because of the diversity and, at times, conflicting needs of different users, given that no single traditional measure is sufficiently powerful to attend adequately to the multiple objectives of divisional performance measurement.

The purpose of this chapter is to examine traditional measures of divisional performance. The first section contains a set of criteria which can be used as a guide in assessing each performance index. This is followed by a discussion of various traditional accounting profit measures, in particular net profit, contribution margin, controllable profit, and sales margin. The next two sections deal with return on investment (ROI) and residual income, where the discussion will focus on some of the measurement problems of using each index, and also on what has become known in the literature as the cost of capital debate. Some of the limitations which are common to all three traditional measures are then considered, followed by a discussion of the use of sales revenue to buttress the use of ROI as an index of divisional performance. The final section provides a summary.

CRITERIA FOR EVALUATION

This section seeks to develop a number of criteria for the evaluation of the various traditional indices of divisional performance which are discussed in this chapter. A general statement would be that a performance index is deemed appropriate as long as it meets the requirements stated under the objectives of divisional performance measurement discussed in Chapter 1. Briefly this would imply attending to the needs of both internal and external users in relation to three main areas: monitoring managerial performance, assessing the profitability of the division both past and future, and guiding divisional managers in making operating decisions. This, however, is too broad a statement to be useful and hence there is need for a more specific set of criteria to guide the evaluation of traditional performance indices.

It could be argued that monitoring managerial performance would require that the performance index should engender corporate-optimal behaviour, promote divisional independence, and maintain the controllability principle (Shillinglaw, 1961). Further, assessment of divisional and corporate profitability requires that the performance index best approximates the "ideal" income measure, if the latter can be identified, as discussed in the previous chapter (see also Tomkins, 1973 and Scapens, 1979).

Corporate optimality

If the benefits of divisionalised structures are to be achieved, in the profit-maximising sense discussed in Chapter 1, then it is essential that individual divisional managers should not be able to take independent actions which maximise their performance index whilst reducing that of the parent company. Sub-optimal behaviour can, and does, arise frequently because of non-cooperative behaviour by individual divisions, but also because of the imperfections in the performance index used (see Solomons, 1965). Examples of the first type include attracting business away from a sister division, and buying or selling products and services externally rather than internally. Such lack of cooperation reflects unfavourably on the performance of other divisions and of the parent company; averting it requires adequate information and the use of administrative enforcement rules. Similar consequences, however, can be caused by the use of an imperfect performance index. The following two examples illustrate the point:

1. Allocation of head office overheads based on divisional sales volume could motivate divisions to seek a lower volume of high-price sales in preference to maximising sales revenue, because savings in overhead allocations more than compensate for reduction in revenues.

2. Under an absorption costing method, where there is no interest charge on capital, divisional managers can increase their profits by building up inventories, and hence can carry forward part of this year's overhead to next year.

As Solomons (1965) has pointed out, these problems arise because of failure to charge divisions the "true" cost to the company of their actions; the true cost of administrative services in the first example, and of using capital in the second example. But such "true" costs are frequently difficult to ascertain and this may explain practitioners' preference for opting for the "easy" option.

It is important to note at the outset, however, that the notion of corporate optimality is problematic because it is based on the restrictive assumption that organisations have clear, consistent, and well-ordered goals. To the extent that goals are multiple, conflicting, and ambiguous, concepts such as corporate optimality and goal congruence become meaningless (see Parker, 1979; Ezzamel and Hart, 1987). As modern organisation theory is supportive of the presence of these problematics with respect to organisational goals, it should be borne in mind that corporate optimality may be an unattainable attribute in most large and diverse corporations, such as those which are typically organised along the multidivisional structure.

Divisional independence

Shillinglaw (1961) has suggested that each division's performance index should be as independent as possible of the efficiency and managerial decisions relating to other parts of the organisation. This is likely to be the case if the firm is a holding company where the divisions would be loosely coupled and where head office plays a minimum role in coordinating divisional activities. But, as indicated in Chapter 1, this structure is far from optimal. Some level of interdependence between each division and head office is assumed in the pure M-form, and interdivisional dependence will arise in the mixed and corrupt multidivisional forms through internal transfers of goods and services. These are organisation design issues which have to be planned carefully.

But divisional independence can be violated by accounting rules, such as those relating to the allocation of central overheads. For example, if such overheads are allocated on the basis of actual divisional sales, the allocation to one division will be higher, even when its own sales revenue is held constant, if the sales of one (or more) division(s) are reduced. Similarly, increases in the levels and scope of corporate-wide expenses, such as research and development, will inevitably increase divisional share of overheads, thereby rendering divisional performance more dependent upon other parts of the organisation.

The controllability principle

One of the main pillars of responsibility accounting is the controllability principle. In the context of divisional accounting this implies that the performance index of each division should reflect all items which are substantially under the control of the divisional manager or divisional staff. The controllability principle is strongly linked to the two previous criteria. Thus, to the extent that headquarters impose administrative enforcement rules to motivate divisional behaviour in a particular direction, for example to buy internally rather than externally, the controllability principle will be impeded *unless* the manager is not made responsible for the consequence of internal purchasing. Similarly, increases in overheads allocated to a particular division because of changes in activity levels, sales or production in other divisions should be excluded when assessing the performance of that manager.

There is, however, some evidence drawn from case studies which indicates that at times firms hold managers accountable for some uncontrollable factors (Merchant, 1989). Examples include: (a) uncontrollable but relevant cost and revenue factors, such as interest expenses and income, and the cost of centralised administration; (b) economic and competitive conditions such as business cycles and price competition; and (c) acts of nature such as accidents and earthquakes. The arguments for making managers accountable for uncontrollable events include motivating them to pay attention to events such as those under (a), encouraging them to respond to events such as those under (b), and helping them to minimise the one-time damage caused by events such as those under (c).

It is important to note that most accounting-based measures of performance or profitability are short-term orientated. A critical issue then in evaluating any short-term performance measure is to examine the extent to which its maximisation is consistent with the maximisation of the ideal income measure discussed in the next chapter. A useful illustration of this is offered by Tomkins (1973), as shown in Figure 2.1.

It is clear from Figure 2.1 that in terms of consistency with ideal income, short-term profit *A* is preferred to short-term profit *B*, since the maxima of *A*, but not of *B*, corresponds to the maxima of ideal income, even though short-term profit *B* is closer in absolute level to ideal income. Hence, in maximising short-term profit *A*, the divisional manager will also be maximising ideal income. However, once the differing needs of the multitude of users of divisional accounting information are considered, the choice becomes much less clear-cut. Whilst short-term profit *A* is preferable for guiding operating and monitoring decisions, it

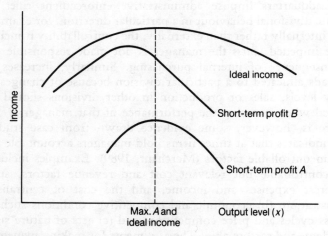

FIGURE 2.1 Short-run profit approximisation of ideal income. Source: C. Tomkins, *Financial Planning in Divisionalised Companies*, (1973), Prentice-Hall. Reprinted with permission.

could be argued that short-term profit B is more useful for the purposes of estimating the economic potential of the division.

TRADITIONAL ACCOUNTING PROFIT

The use of traditional accounting profit as a measure of divisional performance appears to be widespread both in North America and in the UK, although it is by no means the most widely used measure. While it is difficult to derive precise figures from published surveys, because of the use of multiple indices by the same firm, it appears that approximately 40 per cent of a large sample of USA companies used accounting profit (along with other measures such as return on investment or residual income) to assess the performance of divisions and of their managers (Mauriel and Anthony, 1966) compared with 25 per cent in the UK (Tomkins, 1973). Although these statistics are somewhat dated, more 'recent' evidence (e.g. Vancil, 1979) suggests that accounting profit is still being used by many divisionalised companies, particularly those which are organised along the profit-centre basis.

Further, the use of accounting profit in the context of divisional performance has been advocated by some academics, in particular by Shillinglaw (1957) and Amey (1969a; 1969b; 1975). Arguing from the position of macroeconomic efficiency, rather than that of the efficiency of a single enterprise, Amey contends that firms should simultaneously maximise profits and minimise total costs. He argues that by more careful specification of required data it would be possible to produce profit figures which would be a good proxy for economic efficiency. This would involve setting profit targets, measured *ex ante* (that is before the beginning of the period) in economic terms, against which actual profits might be compared. Decision-making and performance evaluation are thus kept, as far as possible, in line with economic efficiency.

Shillinglaw (1957) discussed the usefulness of four variants of accounting profit for the purposes of divisional performance measurement: sales margin, controllable profit, contribution margin, and net profit. For convenience, they are considered in reverse order here.

Net profit appears to be the least useful of the four profit measures. The arbitrary allocation of head office overheads violates the criteria of corporate optimality, divisional independence and event controllability. This is likely to remain the case, despite recent attempts to use activity-based costing systems in which cost drivers are more carefully identified and used for determining the amounts of overheads to be allocated (see, for example, Johnson and Kaplan, 1987). This is because such allocations distort divisional profitability by making it a function of decisions taken outside the division. Further, overhead allocation can result in sub-optimal decisions, if divisions attempt to recover their share of overheads in product prices. Yet these allocations can be useful in approximating relevant but unobservable costs, and can facilitate top management's control over divisional perquisites (e.g. Zimmerman, 1979; Ezzamel and Bourn, 1988) by drawing managerial attention to these costs.

Contribution margin (sales revenue less divisional variable costs and divisional separable, controllable and non-controllable fixed costs) is useful in indicating the amount a division contributes towards the recovery of central overheads. However, like net profit, it is frequently unhelpful for current operating decisions and for monitoring decisions, because divisions are charged for divisional separable non-controllable fixed costs. Such costs are "sunk costs" and are usually initiated by decisions made by higher-level managers.

Controllable profit (sales revenue less divisional variable costs and divisional separable controllable fixed costs) seems particularly useful for evaluating the performance of divisional managers, because it emphasises traceability and controllability.

Sales margin (sales revenue less variable costs) is useful in showing the effects of current decisions, for example changing the selling price by a given amount, on divisional performance (Henderson and Dearden, 1966).

However, irrespective of the specific arguments for or against each of the above four profit variants, traditional accounting profit has several serious limitations. Some of these limitations are shared with both ROI and residual income, and will be discussed later in the chapter; others are considered now. One major criticism of accounting profit is its failure to account for the cost of capital resources entrusted to divisions in those cases where divisional managers have considerable control over the determination of their levels of investment. This can induce sub-optimal decisions by encouraging divisional managers to invest extra capital as long as it can generate a greater than zero return, even though that return may be lower than the company's cost of capital (Solomons, 1965). Moreover, divisions may be encouraged to produce apparent, rather than real, improvements in their efficiency by substituting capital services for labour services in an uneconomic fashion that is difficult for top management to detect (Ezzamel and Hart, 1987).

These limitations arise from the incompatibility of short-term profit maximisation with the maximisation of ideal income. Tomkins (1973) has argued that for accounting profit to be the same as ideal income, two conditions must be satisfied. Firstly, the aggregate of all individual assets and liabilities shown in the balance sheet must be equal to the present value of the firm's net receipts. Secondly, adjustments to assets and liabilities must be reflected in the profit calculation. Given current accounting conventions, it is unlikely that these two conditions will be met.

RETURN ON INVESTMENT (ROI)

The discussion in the preceding section would seem to indicate that variants of accounting profit can be useful measures of divisional performance when the divisions are designed as profit centres, because in this case divisional managers are only responsible for the flows of costs and revenues, but not for the flow of capital. In situations where it is more appropriate to design divisions as investment centres, as is usually the case, performance measures must reflect divisional managers' responsibility not only for profit but also for investment. ROI has been advocated as an appropriate measure of performance in these situations.

The use of ROI for monitoring performance was apparently pioneered by Du Pont, the integrated multi-activity firm. Later

ROI was adapted by General Motors to suit its multidivisional structure. Whilst in a multi-activity firm ROI tends to be used to centralise the allocation of capital among the various activities, divisionalised firms would seek to use ROI to delegate to its divisional managers responsibility for the efficient use of capital. This latter facility is possible because ROI summarises divisional activities in a manner which highlights the contribution of each division to corporate-wide profitability, and this can be manipulated using capital allocations and reward schemes so as to make it conform to corporate objectives. In this sense, ROI makes it possible for the divisionalised firm to play the dual role of capital market and managerial labour market (Johnson and Kaplan, 1987).

The results of empirical research attest to the popularity of ROI both in the USA and the UK. For example, the Mauriel and Anthony (1966) survey revealed that 80 per cent of their sample made use of ROI, and of these 60 per cent used it as the only measure of divisional performance. In the UK, Tomkins' (1973) study revealed that approximately 40 per cent of his sample used ROI both for evaluating the performance of divisional managers and for assessing the performance of the divisions.

The case for ROI is not without theoretical foundations. Gabor and Pearce (1952), for example, have argued that equilibrium for an economic entity is achieved when ROI is maximised. Assuming perfect competition, when the industry is in equilibrium, each firm maximises its return (i.e. earns the normal return on capital) at the level of output which corresponds to minimum average cost. When the industry is in disequilibrium, extra units of the same size should be set up to absorb abnormal profits. Gabor and Pearce have also extended their conclusions to imperfect market settings.

If divisional managers have significant influence over the allocation of central resources, then maximising ROI is unlikely to be consistent with maximising absolute profit, except if divisional investment is constant. As Amey (1969a; 1969b) has argued, it is difficult to think of many situations in which capital is constant, for even if divisional capital is determined by top management, decisions concerning its use, for example changes in activity level, will frequently change its value.

Despite its widespread use in practice, and its appeal to some academics, ROI has several crucial limitations. Calculation of ROI is usually based on the conventions governing the measurement of traditional accounting profit, and hence all shortcomings inherent in such a measurement system would be present. Dearden (1961), Mauriel and Anthony (1966) and Vatter (1959) have documented some of the limitations of ROI when either gross book value (original cost) or net book value is used to determine the investment base. Sub-optimal divisional behaviour can be promoted under both methods in connection with asset replacement decisions and inventory decisions. For example, when gross book value is used to determine the divisional investment base there is an incentive for divisional managers to prematurely scrap equipment which is temporarily idle in the short term, in order to maximise their ROI. When net book value is used, divisional ROI can be biased upwards, especially if the divisional asset portfolio contains a large number of old but serviceable assets, whose original costs are significantly below their replacement costs. This can result in misallocation of company resources if the exaggerated ROI is instrumental in influencing the level of resources committed to each division. It is also possible that divisional managers become reluctant to invest in projects which are profitable but have a lower ROI, because this would result in a lower overall ROI for the division (Dearden, 1960).

In addition, the allocation of receivables, payables and cash, etc. by top management to determine divisional investment base is usually quite arbitrary. Because of the effects of inflation, ROI also exaggerates the success of a division, or conceals possible failings, because money profits are likely to increase in amount at a faster rate than the investment base (Vatter, 1959; Dearden, 1969).

These limitations prompted Horngren (1962) to suggest that the change in the rate of return is often more significant than its absolute size and hence such changes should be the focus of attention in the context of performance evaluation. Amey (1969a; 1969b) has also suggested that it may be expedient to set profit maximisation as the objective and merely express the results as a rate of return. These suggestions, however, introduce only cosmetic changes into the use of ROI as a measure of divisional performance; the main limitations discussed above remain unaddressed.

RESIDUAL INCOME

Mauriel and Anthony (1966) have reported that 27 per cent of their sample use residual income as the only measure of divisional income in the USA, and Tomkins (1973) has reported a similar percentage of UK companies using residual income in *addition* to other measures. Residual income represents the excess of net earnings over the cost of capital and is therefore a measure of performance for investment centres. Variants of residual income similar to those derived for accounting profit can be calculated and used in different decision contexts (see Solomons, 1965).

Several researchers have argued that the use of residual income as a measure of divisional performance would overcome the limitations documented under accounting profit and ROI. Solomons (1965) has argued that charging cost of capital to divisions would fulfil the dual role of guiding decisions and evaluating performance. Hence, divisional managers would have an incentive to invest in all projects that promise internal rates of return higher than, or at least equal to, the cost of capital. No profitable projects would be avoided, as under ROI, and no inefficient investments (in the sense of having expected returns below the cost of capital) would be encouraged, as might be the case under accounting profit. Residual income also facilitates comparisons of the performance of company divisions, as divisional managers would have to cover the cost of capital charged on their investment levels. Under residual income, the actions of divisional managers are made sensitive to changes in capital markets by manipulating divisional required rates of return as the company's cost of capital changes (Shwayder, 1970). Finally, residual income is a better approximation to ideal income than either accounting profit or ROI. Solomons (1965) has suggested that residual income is the short-run analogue of maximising the long-run discounted cash flow (DCF) of the firm. Similarly, Scapens (1979) has shown that a policy of maximising economic profit will result in optimal decisions (in the sense of maximising the net present value of an economic entity) and that economic profit has the characteristics of residual income. Similar conclusions were also reached by other researchers (e.g. Tomkins, 1975; Emmanuel and Otley, 1976).

The question of whether residual income represents an optimal, and practicable, measure of divisional performance led to the emergence of a lively academic debate in the 1970s. The debate centred around whether an explicit inclusion of an imputed cost of capital charge in the calculation of a divisional performance index, as is the case under residual income, is economically sound; this debate came to be known as the cost of capital debate.

The cost of capital debate

It has been pointed out that if the goal of the firm is profit maximisation, and if the cost of capital charges do not affect divisional prices, then the level of activity at which residual income is maximised will in general be smaller than the level at which profit is maximised (because of the higher total costs under residual income). Only in the unlikely case of the cost curve shifting iso-elastically, i.e. the cost curves under both residual income and traditional profit having the same slope in the region of profit-maximising output, will the two activity levels coincide. Thus, charging cost of capital can lead to sub-optimal use of company resources.

This argument may be taken to imply that under profit maximisation the cost of capital should not be treated as part of the total cost. Indeed, Gabor and Pearce (1952) have suggested, in respect of individual firms, that the inclusion of the cost of capital in the total cost curve is incorrect for theoretical and practical reasons. Firstly, they have argued, traditional economic theory does not distinguish between the two fundamental functions of the entrepreneur: provision of money capital and management. In seeking to draw this distinction they define costs as payments to contracting factors, including payments (salaries and compensation) to management, who offer their services at an agreed price. Profit is defined as what remains from the revenues after meeting such costs, and therefore represents a residue to be distributed to controlling factors (providers of capital). The opportunity cost of capital (normal profit under some restrictive assumptions) is a part of that residue. Secondly, Gabor and Pearce pointed out that according to accounting practice, the cost of equity capital is not treated as a cost element but rather as a profit to be distributed amongst ordinary shareholders.

Assuming that management remuneration is included when calculating traditional accounting profit, ROI, and residual income, optimal investment levels under each of these three profitability indices can be determined. To do so, define the condition for maximising traditional accounting profit as:

$$MR = MC^* \qquad (2.1)$$

and the condition for maximising ROI as:

$$\frac{F(X)}{MF(X)} = \frac{R(X) - C^*(X)}{MR(X) - MC^*(X)} \qquad (2.2)$$

and finally, the condition for maximising residual income as:

$$MR = MC^* + MK^* \qquad (2.3)$$

where:

MR is the marginal revenue

MC^* is the marginal cost excluding the opportunity cost of capital

$F(X)$ is the capital requirement as a function of output

$R(X)$ is total revenue as a function of output

$C^*(X)$ is total cost as a function of output, excluding cost of capital

$MF(X)$, $MR(X)$, $MC^*(X)$ are corresponding derivatives

MK^* is the marginal cost of capital.

Figure 2.2 seeks to capture the implications of equations (2.1), (2.2) and (2.3) on investment decisions by showing the optimal investment levels under each of the performance indices; these correspond to: $O\hat{A}$ under traditional accounting profit, OA under ROI, and $O\bar{A}$ under residual income (or marginal approach). The relationships between these three investment levels are:

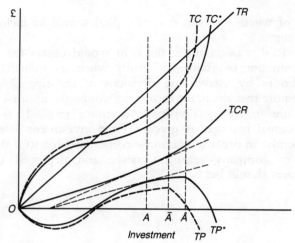

Legend:
TC   : Total cost including the opportunity cost of capital
TC* : Total cost excluding the opportunity cost of capital
TR   : Total revenue
TCR : Total capital requirements
TP   : Total profits when TC is the total cost
TP* : Total profit when TC* is the total cost
Â   : Optimal investment level under accounting profit
Ā   : Optimal investment level under residual income
A   : Optimal investment level under ROI

FIGURE 2.2 Investment levels under alternative profitability measures.

$$OA < O\bar{A} < O\hat{A} \qquad (2.4)$$

That is, the investment level under ROI would be less than that under residual income, and each of these two would be less than the investment level under traditional accounting profit. Except in very special circumstances, relationship (2.4) will normally hold. For example, the relationship $OA = O\bar{A}$ may exist if the cost of capital, K^* increases sharply immediately after OA, such that $MR = MC^* + MK^*$ holds only at OA. Also, the relationship $O\bar{A} = O\hat{A}$ may obtain if the slope of TC^* is the same as that of TC in the region of profit maximisation, that is, if TC^* shifts iso-elastically. The knowledge of which of these three investment levels is the "correct" one would depend to a large extent on the question of whether or not cost of capital should be included in the cost curve.

Under ROI maximisation, the firm would obtain the largest possible amount of abnormal profits when its industry is in disequilibrium by establishing divisions of the size *OA*. This would require that the headquarters determine the optimal size of each of the company divisions according to (2.2), so that each divisional manager is given a fixed investment level *OA*. Consequently, in order to maximise corporate-wide ROI the total amount of company resources raised and deployed by the headquarters should be:

$$\sum_{j=1}^{m} OA_j$$

Thus there would be no spare company resources for divisional managers to compete for. If this approach is to be followed, there would be no need for an imputed cost of capital to be levied against divisions. However, this does not necessarily eliminate the need for calculating the cost of capital, since this is useful in deciding whether or not it is worthwhile for the amount OA_j to be kept tied up in the activities of any particular division.

If, however, the Gabor and Pearce approach is not accepted, and if companies in practice give substantial discretion to divisional managers in determining their investment levels, then it would seem that charging a cost of capital is justifiable in order to ensure that the company does at least cover its cost of capital.

However, criticisms of charging divisions for the cost of capital they utilise have been made by Amey (1969a; 1969b). Firstly, he has argued that charging cost of capital, as suggested by Solomons, does, in fact, confuse investment considerations with production considerations. In evaluating investment proposals, the cost of funds available for investment should be considered. However, determination of the efficient production set, he argues, does not depend on levying a cost of capital charge, but rather on relevant technological possibilities, e.g. scale of production. Once this is solved, economic factors (e.g. relative input prices), rather than *ex post* imputed cost of capital, are the relevant variables to consider before deciding upon which techniques to employ. Secondly, Amey is critical of Solomons' assertion that the cost of capital can fulfil the dual role of guiding decisions and appraising performance. He has argued that, in considering how funds should be allocated between divisions, it is the opportunity cost of uncommitted money capital that is relevant. Once investment has occurred, however, decisions will not be concerned with evaluating performance but rather with the best use to which assets should be put, in which case the opportunity cost of capital goods will be relevant.

Amey's argument in connection with capital cost charges has been associated with much confusion and debate in the accounting literature. Some writers (e.g. Tomkins, 1975) have attempted to reconcile the arguments of Amey and Solomons by suggesting that each is concerned with different problems: Solomons with motivational aspects of project-selection decisions and Amey with appraising divisional performance, given that the investment decision has already been taken. Bromwich (1973) has also suggested that Amey's argument implies that charging an imputed cost of capital is irrelevant for marginal decisions since marginal cost, as it is normally defined, already includes all costs associated with additional output. Amey (1975), however, has rejected both these attempts to reconcile his views with those of Solomons.

Amey's argument was made somewhat clearer in his 1975 paper. In defining costs associated with capital inputs he has distinguished between cash outlay costs (explicit costs) and opportunity costs (implicit costs). Cash outlay costs represent interest payment on debt for working capital and maintenance expenditure for fixed capital. Opportunity costs reflect economic depreciation (including obsolescence) for fixed capital. Interest payment on working capital is treated by Amey as part of this cost function, representing a variable cost paid to contracting factors (money lenders). In the case of new investments, the cost of funds available for investment should be taken into consideration, because it represents the opportunity cost of investing. Once investment decisions have been taken, divisions should be charged with the cost of holding and using the assets, in this case maintenance expenditure and economic depreciation.

One issue that is relevant to the above debate is the extent of autonomy granted to divisions with regard to investment decisions. Solomons addressed cases in which divisional managers have some considerable influence on resource allocation. Amey, however, argues that in the interest of corporate optimality, divisional autonomy with respect to determining divisional investment levels should be limited. Available empirical evidence seems to be consistent with this contention (e.g. NICB, 1961; Tomkins, 1973; Ezzamel and Hilton, 1980a; 1980b, but see Scapens and Sale, 1981, for evidence of greater divisional autonomy in this area, and also refer to the discussion in Chapter 4). In such situations, it may be argued that charging cost of capital to divisions is not justified.

Another related issue is whether maximising residual income is compatible with maximising the net present value of the firm. Although Solomons contends that the two concepts are consistent, Amey argues that they are not, essentially because the *imputed* cost of capital suggested by Solomons is not always the correct cost of capital to consider, as argued above. Flower (1971) has suggested a reconciliation between residual income and DCF. Under Flower's scheme, residual income figures are calculated using DCF principles for valuing assets, depreciation and interest charges (see the discussion in Chapter 3). Given that annual net cash flow is made up of depreciation and interest on capital (normal profit), the target residual income for divisional managers under Flower's scheme will always be zero. To instruct a divisional manager to meet a zero residual income target may not induce the desired motivational consequences, since many divisional managers are likely to find it difficult to identify with a "zero" performance target (see Bromwich, 1973, for a discussion of the adverse motivational consequences of such a measure). Tomkins (1975) demonstrated that Solomons' argument holds when multi-period effects are absent: i.e. when each period begins and ends without working capital balances, and current output decisions have no effect on future cash flows. Adjustments for multi-period effects, Tomkins argues, can simply be introduced into the non-multi-period effects model by allowing for the carrying forward of working capital balances. Amey (1975) criticises Tomkins' argument, on the grounds that once we consider multi-period effects it is not helpful to concentrate on any one period in isolation, because of likely interactions between different periods.

Moreover, as Amey points out, it is not only the past which may interact with the present; the future may interact with the present and the present with the future.

The above discussion indicates the problematic nature of the debate on the cost of capital in the context of divisional accounting. The debate is far from resolved and is likely to continue, as long as discussion is constrained within the confines of the three traditional performance indices so far considered.

SOME COMMON LIMITATIONS OF THE ABOVE THREE INCOME INDICES

We have specified the limitations as decision-making tools for divisionalised organisations of each of traditional accounting profit, ROI, and residual income. There are also certain limitations shared by all three indices as a result of their common use of conventional accounting measurement techniques. These limitations are summarised below.

Short-run measurement problems

Divisional managers can in the short-run exploit the weaknesses of conventional accounting measurement techniques to produce reported profits above "real" profits. Examples of such manipulations include:

1. Arranging for the transfer of reported divisional income from one accounting period to another, e.g. by the overstatement of assets or revenues and the understatement of liabilities or costs. Notice that this sort of manipulation should have no effect on the present value of the division or of its parent.
2. Cutting down some expenditures with potential services extending over more than one accounting period; examples of this are R&D, personnel training, public relations, etc. This type of manipulation will tend to reduce the present value of the division and the parent company, assuming that the level of expenditure was initially optimal.

3. Choosing strategies (e.g. investment projects) which yield high expected returns in the short-run, but which are non-optimal so far as their net present values (NPVs) are concerned. This type of action has a negative effect on the present value of the division and the parent company, although such effects may be concealed in the short-run.

These three examples demonstrate that any short-run income index based on conventional accounting measurement techniques need not be consistent with the long-run profitability as formulated in terms of NPV.

Decision-making needs and lack of future orientation

Extensive comments appear in the literature in respect of the backward rather than forward-looking view of conventional accounting measurement techniques. Decision-making requires forward estimates, however. If the future is not reflected in the past, historical records may be unhelpful or misleading. The decision to continue or abandon a division has very little to do with historical divisional income, unless what has happened in the past will be repeated, or at least gives a good indication of what is likely to happen in the future. One particularly dubious convention in this context is that of the "going concern", when it underlies an income figure which is then used to justify the "termination" of a division.

The problem of sub-optimal divisional behaviour

Divisional goals are usually assumed to be derived from those of the parent company. Unless each division is highly independent, and exogenous, with respect to every other division, or unless decision-making is centralised, conflicts between divisional and central goals will inevitably arise. These conflicts would arise because a divisional manager would be tempted to select those alternatives which generate the highest profit or come closest to achieving some particular divisional target, irrespective of their effects on other divisions and on the parent company, thereby violating the criteria of corporate optimality and divisional independence. This is another problem which traditional accounting measurement techniques fail to solve, because they do not consider the effects of the actions of a divisional manager on other company divisions.

The preceding discussion has focused on identifying two sets of limitations which reduce the usefulness of traditional accounting indices as measures of divisional performance: (a) index-specific limitations, and (b) commonly shared limitations. Taken together, these limitations indicate that only under highly restrictive assumptions will the maximisation of any of these indices correspond to the maximisation of ideal income as reflected in discounted cash flow terms. In the following section we examine an additional traditional measure of performance, sales revenue, and explore the extent to which its use alongside other traditional indices attenuates these limitations.

SALES REVENUE AS A PERFORMANCE MEASURE

Examination of the results of empirical studies and of the findings of business history reveal two important lessons relating to the practice of divisionalised companies. Firstly, companies frequently use multiple measures of divisional profitability (see, for example, Mauriel and Anthony, 1966; Tomkins, 1973) and therefore appear to be less obsessed than academics with the pursuit of the elusive *single* optimal measure of profitability. Secondly, companies frequently make use of other financial, non-profit measures of performance; for example, sales revenue and market share, and hence appear to be fully aware of the limitations of relying exclusively on profitability measures.

One particularly telling example of the latter approach relates to the practices of the pioneering multidivisional organisation General Motors (GM). As indicated earlier, GM borrowed the idea of ROI from the vertically integrated Du Pont Powder Company and adapted it to suit its divisionalised structure. GM's policy was *not* to simply seek to earn the highest attainable ROI, irrespective of other financial indicators. Rather, the objective was to earn

the highest long-run ROI consistent with sound growth of the
business expressed in attainable volume. More precisely, the
objective was to achieve 20 per cent after-tax ROI, while
operating on average at 80 per cent of standard capacity (Johnson
and Kaplan, 1987).

Further, in order to facilitate the co-ordination of divisional
annual operating plans with long-term ROI and standard capacity
policies, GM invented a unique system that came to be known
as the "price study". Each divisional manager had to prepare a
price study for the next year, which typically had three basic
elements: (a) a forecast of operations based on the following year's
expected volume, (b) a forecast of operations based on standard
volume, and (c) a determination of each product's standard price,
"that is the price which, with the plant operating at standard
volume, would produce the adjudged normal average rate of
return on capital which has been referred to as the economic
return attainable" (Bradley, 1926, p. 7). The forecast at expected
volume and the standard prices were used to assess divisional *ex-
ante* operating programmes in terms of GM's policy regarding
long-run financial policy. The forecast at standard volume was
used to monitor division current operations.

It is instructive to examine this scheme in more detail (see
Brown, 1924; Bradley, 1926; Sloan, 1963; Johnson, 1978; Johnson
and Kaplan, 1987). Initially, each divisional manager prepared for
each product a forecast of selling price and sales volume. Proposed
selling prices had to be consistent with current year's prices and
competitors' expected prices. In preparing these forecasts, divisions
were assisted by central office statistics showing GM's estimated
share of the national market in each division's price range.
Subsequently, divisional managers estimated operating costs,
capital requirements, and ROI, using as a basis data on past ratios
of costs to output and investment to output. From all this data,
forecast ROI for the coming year was derived. To ensure that
divisional forecast prices and ROI were consistent with GM's
long-run financial plan, top management compared proposed
prices with the relevant standard price, the latter being the factory-
delivered price that had to be charged at standard volume (80 per
cent) in order to earn the standard ROI (20 per cent). If the two
prices were consistent, top management would be confident that

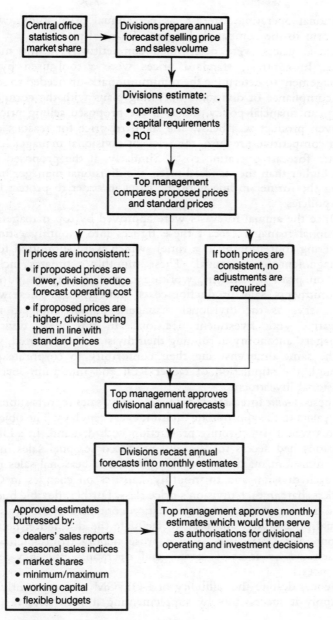

FIGURE 2.3 General Motors price study.

divisional operating forecast, as per annual price study, would conform to the company's long-run financial plan.

Actual prices were determined competitively in the market place. In contrast, standard prices were a tool used by top management to determine the minimum mark-up needed to secure the compliance of divisional operating plans with the company's long-run financial policy. Thus, if the proposed selling price for a given product was below the standard price for reasons other than competitive pressure, the relevant divisional manager had to reduce forecast operating costs. Similarly, if the proposed price was higher than the standard price, the divisional manager had to bring the former in line with the latter in order to protect long-run policies.

Once the annual forecasts were approved by top management, divisional managers recast these figures into monthly estimates (covering four months at a time), which were submitted to top management for approval. These monthly estimates included data on plant investment, working capital, inventory, purchase commitments, sales production costs, and earnings. These would then serve as the divisional manager's authorisation to make operating and investment decisions. In this way, divisional managers' autonomy in running their divisions was assured, while at the same time ensuring their conformity to corporate goals through the stipulation of target ROI and minimum levels of divisional investment.

These *ex-ante* forecasts were buttressed by sales reports submitted by dealers to the appropriate division every ten days. The objective of this was to synchronise production with demand. In addition, divisions had access to centrally produced seasonal sales indices and minimum/maximum working capital to seasonal sales ratios for each division and to monthly statistics on changes in GM's market share in each division's price class. Further, flexible budgets were developed, from the information contained in the divisional annual price study, and used to facilitate the distinction between output-related variances, which arose mainly from fluctuations in demand or forecast errors, and operating efficiency-related variances.

Hence, despite the fallibility of ROI, GM was apparently able to apply it successfully by supplementing it with sales revenue, sales reports, and flexible budgets. In this respect, Johnson and Kaplan (1987, pp. 115–16) have argued:

> GM's return on investment criterion for judging divisional financial performance apparently provided proper motivation, then, for division managers to pursue top management's goals. Further motivation was supplied by the timely and accurate reporting of divisional financial performance to GM's top management. The return on investment data sent to top management related each division's performance directly to top-level goals. The data were prepared in all divisions according to company-wide accounting standards; they were audited by top management staff personnel; they were compiled for top management by corporate staff personnel whose company-wide perspective freed them from divisional biases; and they were timely. The data revealed promptly and unambiguously any failure of a division manager to meet the company's basic financial objectives. In so doing, they enabled top management to swiftly remove a division manager who failed to perform as expected.

SUMMARY

In this chapter we have developed a number of criteria which were then used as a guide in assessing the usefulness of several measures of divisional performance. The criteria developed were those relating to (a) corporate optimality, (b) divisional independence, and (c) the controllability principle. The measures of divisional performance considered were traditional accounting profit, ROI, residual income, and sales revenue.

It was suggested that whilst various variants of accounting profit can serve a number of purposes, these measures have several crucial limitations which render them highly problematic indices of divisional performance. Although ROI successfully reduces some of these limitations, in particular by relating profitability to the divisional investment base, it still suffers from several serious limitations. Residual income has gained the support of many academics on the grounds of its compatibility with ideal income and its responsiveness to capital market changes through the cost of capital calculations. However, as indicated in the chapter, there are two main problems with these arguments. The first is that the debate relating to whether or not it is sensible for a cost of capital to be charged in the calculation of residual income is far from settled. Second, even if some consensus can be reached among academics with regard to the cost of capital debate, residual income, in common with accounting profit and ROI, still has several limitations specifically relating to its emphasis on short-term performance and on *ex post* information (that is after an event has taken place).

If the conceptually superior DCF measures of divisional performance can be used, then many of the above problems will be averted, or at the very least minimised. However, the use of DCF is not widespread in practice, presumably because of the difficulties associated with operationalising it, as will be discussed in Chapter 3. We may therefore have to be left with conventional performance measures, such as those discussed in this chapter. The use of multiple financial measures (as evidenced by the practices of the pioneering GM and many other companies) as well as non-financial and qualitative measures would appear to be the second-best alternative available. The roles of these other measures in the context of divisional performance evaluation will be examined in detail later in the book, but before we do so we deal in the next chapter with non-traditional measures of divisional performance.

QUESTIONS

1. Discuss the criteria suggested in the literature for the evaluation of alternative measures of divisional performance.
2. Contrast both the theoretical underpinnings and the conceptual and practical limitations relating to the use of accounting profit and return on investment for the purposes of divisional performance measurement.
3. "The use of residual income as a measure of divisional performance overcomes the limitations of both accounting profit and return on investment." Comment.

4. "Charging the cost of capital to divisions fulfils the dual role of guiding decisions and evaluating performance." Comment.
5. "Residual income is the short-run analogue of maximising the long-run discounted cash flow of the firm." Comment.
6. Explain and evaluate the Solomons/Amey debate with respect to levying a cost of capital charge in measuring divisional performance.
7. Describe and evaluate General Motors' price study scheme. To what extent do you think it could be successful in aligning the interests of divisional managers with those of central management?
8. Caswell Bay Ltd.[1]

Caswell Bay Ltd is a multidivision, multiproduct company operating in the electronics industry. The number of different items produced by the industry is fairly large, but broadly speaking they are all grouped under five main product categories. These products are used by a wide variety of manufacturers in both the capital goods and consumer goods industries, and are sold both in the UK and abroad.

The industry as a whole has been having mixed fortunes with regard to the trend of home and overseas sales. During the 1970s, home sales for the industry increased by only 20 per cent as compared with an increase of over 150 per cent in overseas markets. However, during the 1980s, home-market demand became more stationary, and in some years it even fell below the home demand of the previous decade. To make matters worse, the penetration of overseas manufacturers into UK markets increased noticeably during this period. The combined effects of static home demand and increased competition from overseas manufacturers caused several UK companies, including Caswell Bay Ltd, to intensify their search for export markets.

Caswell Bay Ltd is one of the big four companies in the electronics industry. The company has five large manufacturing divisions, and each division produces one of the five main product groups of the electronics industry. Two of these divisions have particularly interesting features.

---

[1] Reprinted with permission from M. Ezzamel, "Caswell Bay Limited", in D. Otley, D. Brown and C. Wilkinson (eds), *Case Studies in Management Accounting*, Prentice-Hall, 1989, pp. 64–7.

The first, the West Midlands division, produces grade I semi-conductors, and sells 80 per cent of its total sales in the home market. The North-East division produces micro-chips, and in contrast 90 per cent of its total sales are made in overseas markets. This is mainly because the company had committed itself to a major capacity-expansion policy in the North-East division as a result of over-optimistic demand forecasts.

The home-market shares for both product groups (products hereafter) produced by the two divisions have been fairly stable for a number of years, although competition in export markets for both products is very strong, and home and foreign competitors produce almost completely identical products.

Cost data and selling prices for the two products, both for home markets and export markets are as in Table 2.1. In 1986, the total sales volume of semi-conductors was 200,000 units, compared with 100,000 units for micro-chips. Capital employed in the West Midlands division was calculated as £30,000,000, compared with £15,000,000 for the North-East division.

The company's main long-run objective is to earn a 'satisfactory' rate of return on capital employed. Consequently, each year every division is set a target rate of return on capital employed, and overheads are allocated to divisions. The overheads allocated tend to vary with the level of divisional profitability.

The pricing decision is highly centralised in the sense that divisions have to follow company guidelines, and the pricing policy

TABLE 2.1 Cost and Price Data (£ per Unit)

	West Midlands (semi-conductors)		North-East (micro-chips)	
	Home Market	Overseas Market	Home Market	Overseas Market
Variable cost	40	40	80	80
Overheads*	40	10	40	10
Total cost	80	50	120	90
Selling price	100	62.5	150	112.5

* Includes Head Office and Group expenses apportioned to divisions.

discriminates between the home market and export markets. In the home market, full cost-plus is used to determine the price, while in the export markets a variant between variable cost-plus and full cost-plus is used as the predominant pricing strategy. In addition, head office or group expenses are apportioned to divisions on the basis of profitability. This all means that divisions have to sell the same product at a higher price in the home market than in overseas markets.

The nature of the markets in which the divisions operate facilitates the application of this price discriminating policy. First, although the industry does not engage in cut-throat competition, there is always scope for competitive pricing strategies. Second, the demand for semi-conductors and micro-chips is derived demand, in the sense that both products are essential elements of much larger products and jobs. This renders the total demand for both products relatively insensitive to 'reasonable' changes in prices. Third, the nature of both products makes it rather difficult for home customers to buy from overseas markets at the lower prices.

The accounting system that has to be used by divisions produces both variable- and full-cost data. However, variable-cost data does not include the 'variable' elements included in so-called 'semi-variable' and 'semi-fixed' costs.

The manager of the West Midlands division has strongly protested against the practice of differential overhead allocation for home and overseas markets. He argues that he has been repeatedly penalised because most of his semi-conductor production is sold in the home market. He further argues that the policy used to apportion head office and group expenses worsens his division's apparent results. West Midlands is more profitable than the North-East division, but this profit-based apportionment of overheads causes his return on capital employed (calculated as net profit divided by capital employed) to be lower than that of the North-East division. Because of these points, he argues that overheads should be either apportioned according to usage of fixed facilities or, better still, completely ignored in calculating divisional rates of return.

The chief accountant, however, takes a different stance. He insists that apportionment of overheads to divisions and products in the home market is essential if the company as a whole is to attain its main objective of earning a 'satisfactory' rate of return on capital employed. He advances four reasons to support his argument. First, semi-conductors are capital intensive, whereas micro-chips are labour intensive. If central overheads are not apportioned then the semi-conductors will attract more company resources, and this will not be an optimal allocation of capital. Second, if central overheads are not apportioned, some managers will make excessive use of central facilities at the expense of other managers. This could result in the disadvantaged managers obtaining inferior internal services or purchasing better services externally at a higher price. Third, full-cost pricing induces desirable stability in prices. Since the price includes an overhead recovery rate which is thought to be appropriate for each product, the uncertainty encountered in determining a sufficiently adequate 'plus' under variable-cost pricing to ensure full overhead recovery is avoided. Fourth, variable-cost pricing does not deal adequately with the unpredictability of costs in the real world. Although many cost items are fixed, their actual levels are not always known in advance.

In the case of export markets the situation is rather different. First, to maintain the company's cutting edge in the highly competitive export markets, the pricing strategy needs to be more flexible. Lower central overhead-recovery rates are therefore allowed to divisions in relation to the value of their export sales. Second, production for the home market is rather different from production for the export markets. In the case of the home market, products are made either to standard units or to fulfil special orders, whereas production for export markets tends to be in large quantities in response to large orders. Hence, in the latter case fixed costs per unit tend to be lower as compared with home-market production. It is, therefore, not unreasonable to charge lower overhead-recovery rates to export production.

(a) Evaluate the arguments put forward by the manager of the West Midlands division and by the chief accountant.

(b) Outline the main implications of the company's pricing policy and the differential overhead-recovery system for the West Midlands and North-East divisions, and for the company as a whole.

(c) Should the manager of the West Midlands division seek to sell as much as possible of his semi-conductors production in overseas markets? What factors should be taken into consideration in deciding on this from the point of view of the division and that of the company?

(d) Indicate what pricing policy you would use if you were the chief accountant in Caswell Bay Ltd.

3

Non-Traditional Financial Measures of Performance

The discussion in Chapter 2 examined the suitability of traditional financial measures for assessing the performance of divisionalised organisations. It was suggested there that these traditional measures suffer from two types of limitation; index-specific limitations and common limitations. Most index-specific limitations can be reduced by the judicious use of multiple indices. Dealing with common limitations, i.e. short-termism, focusing on *ex-post* information, and sub-optimal behaviour, however, requires the use of more radical alternative techniques.

It has long been argued that discounted cash flow techniques offer one such radical approach. Because they emphasise long-termism, *ex-ante* information, and optimal behaviour, several writers argue that discounted cash flow-based income measures should replace traditional accounting measures. But discounted cash flow techniques, while theoretically superior to traditional measures, are not easy to apply in practice, since they require reliable estimates of annual expected cash flows and discount rates over very long periods of time.

The purpose of this chapter is to examine DCF-based income measures of divisional performance. The following sections focus on the relevance of DCF income to the measurement of divisional performance; hence we discuss model assumptions, model formulation, and some challenges to DCF applications, including measures of divisional risk premiums and divisional cost of capital. The final section provides a summary.

DISCOUNTED CASH FLOW (DCF) INCOME – THE BASIC MODEL

Most of the proponents of cash flow accounting have been primarily concerned with its use at company level, either as a replacement for traditional accounting profit (Bodenhorn, 1964 and Lawson, 1971a) or as a complementary reporting technique (Lee, 1972). Furthermore, Lawson (1971b), Flower (1971), and Ezzamel (1979) have suggested a measure of divisional performance based on DCF because it reflects ideal income. In this section, we investigate the usefulness of a DCF measure for divisional accounting purposes, and point out some of the challenges to the DCF technique. To facilitate our discussion, however, we first describe the ideal performance index.

Ideal performance index

Ideal indices of performance are theoretical constructs which are developed to serve as a guide against which workable measures can be assessed. They also serve as a motivating force in guiding our efforts to develop more complete measures of performance. If the main objective of the firm is expressed in terms of profit maximisation, then the "ideal" income concept can be stated as the maximisation of the discounted cash flow (DCF) value of the firm, that is the maximisation of the present value of future net receipts (Solomons, 1965; Tomkins, 1973).

Given this objective, the ideal income measure for division j in period t, Z_{jt}, can be expressed as the difference in the present values of the division at the beginning and end of the period, plus any dividends paid out during the period, less new funds raised externally:

$$Z_t^j = V_t^j - V_{t-1}^j + D_t^j - F_t^j \tag{3.1}$$

where:

V_t^j = the present value of future net cash receipts for division j in period t

D_t^j = dividends paid out during period t

F_t^j = new externally-raised funds.

Model assumptions

The application of DCF to an accounting entity, such as a division, is not usually identical with its application to a capital investment project, because of differences in their life spans. In general, it is more difficult to forecast the life span of a division compared with that of an investment project. In fact, one of the widely accepted conventions in the preparation of financial accounting statements for an accounting entity is the assumption that the entity is a "going concern", i.e. that it has an indefinite life. Given a world without uncertainty, the present value of division j at the end of year 0 may be defined as:

$$PV_{t=0}^j = \sum_{t=1}^{\infty} \frac{C_t^j}{(1 + R_f)^t} \tag{3.2}$$

where:

$PV_{t=0}^j$ = present value of division j in year 0

C_t^j = net cash flow of division j expected in any year (t)

R_f = risk-free interest rate (assumed constant over all periods for simplicity).

In contrast, the present value of an asset, PV^s, with an expected life of n years (where n is a finite number of years) at the end of year 0 is:

$$PV_{t=0}^s = \sum_{t=1}^{n} \frac{C_t^s}{(1 + R_f)^t} \tag{3.3}$$

Normally, in order to survive as a "going concern", a division is credited with the stream of annual capital recovered and so we can expect an indefinite stream of net cash flows. This is not the case with an investment project, as it is not usually credited with such annual capital recovered and consequently its present value declines over time. Given the certainty assumption, the present value of division j at the end of year 1 may be defined as:

$$PV_{t=1}^j = \sum_{t=1}^{\infty} \frac{C^j}{(1 + R_f)^{t-1}} \tag{3.4}$$

or,

$$PV_{t=1}^j = PV_{t=0}^j \cdot (1 + R_f) \tag{3.4a}$$

From (3.4a) we have:

$$PV_{t=1}^j - PV_{t=0}^j = PV_{t=0}^j \cdot (R_f) = \pi_{t=1}^j \tag{3.5}$$

That is, equation (3.5) shows the "normal" profit or opportunity cost of capital, as represented by the discount rate. If the whole of this amount is to be taken for distribution then, *ceteris paribus*, the present value of the division after such distribution takes place will be the same as that at the end of year 0 or:

$$\{PV_{t=1}^j - [PV_{t=0}^j \cdot (R_f)]\} = PV_{t=0}^j \tag{3.6}$$

By definition in the context of discounted cash flow models, annual net cash flow equals annual "normal" profit, π_t, plus annual depreciation, D_t, or

$$C_t = \pi_t + D_t \tag{3.7}$$

From (3.5) and (3.7) we have

$$\pi_{t=1}^j = PV_{t=0}^j \cdot (R_f) = C_{t=1}^j - D_{t=1}^j \tag{3.8}$$

The equality relationship in (3.8) is, therefore, based on two strict assumptions:

(a) that precisely $D_{t=1}^j$ will be retained in the division, and

(b) that $D^j_{t\,=\,1}$ will be reinvested in a project whose discounted value equals $D^j_{t\,=\,1}$. Such would be the case under our assumption of a perfectly certain world.

If $D^j_{t\,=\,1}$ is to be reinvested in a project with a positive net present value – when relaxing the certainty assumption – then,

$$\{PV^j_{t\,=\,1} - [PV^j_{t\,=\,0} \cdot (Rf)]\} > PV^j_{t\,=\,0}$$

Also, if all $\pi^j_{t\,=\,1}$ or part of it were to be retained in business for reinvestment, the present-value curve of the division would increase.[1]

The present-value curve of the division would decrease, however, if the initial investment in the division is reduced and/or if the retained amounts are invested at less than (R_f).

This model can be made slightly more realistic without significantly altering our conclusions by assuming summation of returns over a long, but finite, horizon. Such an adjustment in the model acknowledges our inability to forecast to eternity. Naturally, the model does change, for when forecasting becomes possible with respect to a period that was not forecastable previously, its net cash flows are included in the calculation of divisional present value. For example, if the span of forecasting ability is regarded as fifty years, then at the end of year 0 the present value calculation would be based on a time span of year 1 to year 50. At the end of year 1, the forecasting ability would extend to year 51. Therefore, the present value at the end of year 1 would be made up of the net cash flow of year 1 plus the discounted cash flows of the following fifty years instead of forty-nine years. Despite this, because of annual charges, usual discount rates and long-time horizon, the model is not likely to change significantly from the infinite time horizon model.

DIVISIONAL GOAL MODEL AND DCF

If we relax the assumptions of perfect knowledge and complete certainty about the future, various approaches may be used to

---

[1] The steepness of the present-value curve in this case will depend on how much of $\pi^j_{t\,=\,1}$ is reinvested.

incorporate the DCF technique into a divisional goal model. However, once the assumptions of certainty are relaxed, the model presented above becomes more complicated. Divisional future cash flows will be stochastic and their probability distributions will need to be estimated. Appropriate adjustments taking account of risk will have to be introduced. Writing $E(C_t^j)$ to denote the expected cash flow of division j in period t, Y_t^j as some appropriate certainty equivalent, λ as the price of risk in the market, and $\text{Cov}[C_t^j, \tilde{r}_m]$ as the covariance of the random returns of division j with those of the market portfolio, the present value of division j in period t can be rewritten as:

$$PV_t^j = \sum_t^\infty \frac{Y_t^j E(C_t^j)}{(1 + R_f)^t} = \sum_t^\infty \frac{E(C_t^j) - \lambda\text{Cov}\left[\,C_t^j, \tilde{r}_m\,\right]}{(1 + R_f)^t} \qquad (3.9)$$

with $\lambda = [E(rm) - R_f]/\sigma_{rm}^2$, where $E(R_m)$ is the expected return on the market portfolio, and σ_{rm}^2 is the variance of the market returns.

Alternatively, a risk–adjusted discount rate k_t^j may be used in which case (3.9) can be rewritten as:

$$PV_t^j = \sum_t^\infty \frac{E(C_t^j)}{(1 + k_t^j)^t} \qquad (3.10)$$

The DCF models under uncertainty expressed in (3.9) and (3.10) raise several interesting questions. One such question is how can divisional performance be assessed in DCF terms?

One possible approach would be to instruct the divisional manager at the beginning of the period to maximise the expected end–of–period present value of the division. Writing Z^{*j} to indicate the divisional objective function to be maximised, the *ex-ante* present value target of division j at the end of period ($t = 1$) calculated at the end of period 0 may appear as follows:

$$\text{Maximise } Z^*{}_{t=1}^j = \sum_{t=1}^\infty \frac{E(C_t^j)}{(1 + k_t^j)^{t-1}} \qquad (3.11)$$

The divisional objective in (3.11) can then be compared against the present value of the division calculated at the end of year 1, which we denote $Z^{\prime j}{}_{t=1}$. The expression $Z^{\prime j}{}_{t=1}$ would be made up of two elements:

1. actual net cash flow achieved at the end of period ($t = 1$), denoted $\hat{C}^j_{t=1}$; and
2. new expected future net cash flows, which may differ from those which were expected at the end of the previous period because of actions taken by the divisional manager in the current period, changes in economic conditions, and changes in forecasting ability. These are denoted here as C'^j_t .

Consequently, the recalculated (*ex-post*) present value of division j at end of period ($t = 1$) is:

$$Z'^j_{t=1} = \hat{C}^j_{t=1} + \sum_{t=2}^{\infty} \frac{E(C'^j_t)}{(1 + K^j_t)^{t-1}} \quad (3.12)$$

By comparing (3.12) against (3.11) the efficiency of the divisional manager can be assessed, remembering that the effects on Z'^j caused by variables outside the control of the divisional manager should be isolated.

Theoretically speaking, the division as well as the parent company should be better off if $Z'^j > Z^{*j}$, no matter whether this is due to an increase in actual net cash flow of the last period, e.g. $\hat{C}^j_{t=1} > C^{*j}_{t=1}$, or due to an increase in expected future net cash flows, e.g. $E(C'^j_t) > E(C^{*j}_t)$. This implies that top management would be indifferent as between having a certain amount of net cash flow in the current period or an equivalent discounted value of future net cash flows. However, under uncertainty, top management is not likely to be indifferent. Current net cash flow would usually be preferred to an equivalent discounted value of future net cash flows for two possible reasons:

1. The discount rate may not take full account of the "right" substitution rate between current and future cash flows, owing to the difficulties inherent in calculating divisional risk premium.
2. Given information asymmetry it is frequently the divisional manager's subjective judgement that forms the basis of the estimates of future cash flows. It seems plausible to assume that each divisional manager would have a vested interest in taking an optimistic view of such flows. These estimates cannot be readily checked by central management. The above

goal model does not reflect any such preference as regards current net cash flow.

To avoid this problem, we may incorporate a cash flow concept of income in the divisional goal model, instead of the present value of the division. One version of this is the measure of divisional performance suggested by Flower.

Flower (1971) has proposed a residual income concept based on the DCF technique. Assets should be valued at the end of each period according to the discounted value of their future net cash flows – excluding net cash flows obtained at the end of that period. Depreciation is calculated as the difference between the present value of future cash flows of an asset between two subsequent periods. An interest charge is also computed on the present value of the assets at the beginning of the period. Given that under DCF models annual net cash flow is made of depreciation and interest on capital (normal profit) – equation (3.7), the target residual income a divisional manager is instructed to achieve would always be zero. However, it is not clear in Flower's paper how his recommended concept would be used for measuring divisional performance.

One possible approach would be to compare actual residual income against target residual income for each period. Depreciation in the first period would be the difference between the present value at the beginning of period 1, assuming that the best alternatives were selected, and the present value at the end of that period given the selected alternatives. Interest for period 1 would be based on the present value of the best alternatives. There would be no problem in subsequent periods, as depreciation and interest charges would be based on the present value of the selected alternatives.

Another possible approach to make use of Flower's residual income concept would be to:

1. Compare the net present value of the selected projects with the net present value of the best alternatives just after making the decision.
2. Compare actual residual income with target residual income each period. Depreciation and interest calculation would be based on the present value of the selected projects.

Needless to say, the same results would be obtained under either approach, but is there much point in using a DCF-based residual income for divisional accounting purposes? Results similar to those obtained under the DCF residual income concept can be derived by:

1. Comparing the net present values of the selected alternatives and the best alternatives once the decision is made, and then monitoring the present value of the selected alternatives over time.
2. Comparing periodic target net cash flows with actual net cash flows.

Given the above discussion, the DCF technique can probably best be incorporated in the divisional goal model by instructing the divisional manager to maximise a target net cash flow with a constraint on the minimum present value of the division at the end of the period. This goal model may be expressed as follows:

$$\text{Maximise: } Z^*{}_t^j = E(C^*{}_t^j) \qquad (3.13)$$

$$\text{Subject to: } PV_t^j > \hat{P}V_t^j$$

where $Z^*{}_t^j$, $E(C^*{}_t^j)$, PV_t^j are as before, and

$\hat{P}V_t^j = $ the minimum target present value of division j at end of period t.

By comparing actual net cash flow with target net cash flow, the importance of current cash flow is emphasised. By specifying a constraint on the minimum present value of the division at the end of each period, the divisional manager is discouraged, *ceteris paribus*, from increasing current cash flow at the expense of future cash flows. Under this last model, divisional performance statements need not be complicated by the inclusion of items such as depreciation, income before interest, and residual income, as under the Flower method. Furthermore, the motivational shortcomings of setting a zero residual income target to divisional managers would be avoided (e.g. Bromwich, 1973). The objective function to be maximised in (3.13) is different from the "ideal" income concept expressed in equation (3.1), in the sense that the first incorporates both the latter and the annual depreciation charge

– see equation (3.7). Since we are now considering the use of the above model – (3.13) – in an uncertain world, the determination of $\hat{P}V_i^j$ would be subject to the limitations of forecasting which are implicit under such conditions. These limitations are discussed below.

CHALLENGES TO DCF APPLICATIONS

In a theoretical sense, it is quite possible that the incorporation of DCF in the divisional goal model could be used to solve most of the problems associated with traditional accounting measurement (these were discussed in detail in the previous chapter). However, DCF techniques have been subjected to criticism. The main criticisms are discussed below.

First, there is the problem of uncertainty and the extent of reliability of cash flow forecasts. It is often argued that forecasting techniques have improved in the last few decades (see Chambers, Mullick, and Smith 1971), but they are by no means perfect, and by the nature of the world never can be. It is also impossible for central management to forecast cash flows of every possible alternative facing the division. Hence, the subjectivity of DCF income should at least be borne in mind when assessing managerial performance. If the net cash flow expectations of a divisional manager are different from those of central management, it is usually difficult, if not impossible, to establish whose expectations are correct.

Second, some writers have expressed concern over the treatment of depreciation under DCF. Jaedicke (1967) makes the point that cash flows do not distinguish between return *on* capital and return *of* capital. The DCF technique does not treat depreciation explicitly. However, the recovery of depreciation equivalent is included in the annual net cash flow – equation (3.7). But, the point remains that the recovered depreciation equivalent has no logical relationship with physical depreciation of the assets involved. The implicit depreciation follows the pattern of annual net cash flow – increasing with it and decreasing with it. In terms of NPV, an asset might appreciate instead of depreciating for some years, simply because annual net cash flows in these years are very small, and hence they are more than compensated for by the mechanics of discounting for periods nearer to the end of the asset life span. There are no guarantees that such appreciation in the NPV of an asset reflects a genuine increase in its economic value.

Third, there is the question of timing the allocation of income. Under DCF, the NPV of a project is considered to belong to the period in which the project is accepted. The point could be made that such income belongs not only to that period, but also extends to the full time horizon covered by the implementation of the decision. However, counter arguments in this respect are possible. For example, it could be argued that the conventional pattern of allocation is sensible, since the selection of a project with a positive NPV may be dependent upon the timing of the decision.

Fourth, there is the problem of how the discount rate should be determined. This is a twofold problem of measuring not only the time preference of money but also the corresponding risk class of the division concerned. Time preference will vary from person to person, depending upon their own views of the world, and it is usually assumed that the aggregate of their various preferences will be reflected appropriately in the time preference of the economic entity concerned.

The other side of the problem is whether to use one discount rate for all divisions, or to use different discount rates, depending on the risk class of the activities of individual divisions. Solomons (1965, pp. 158–9) and Flower (1971, p. 207) have suggested using the company cost of capital as a unique discount rate for all divisions.[2] This incorporates two implicit assumptions:

1. If this procedure is to provide the appropriate incentives, the preferences of the divisional managers should coincide with those of top management. This would imply that the personal rate of time preference of each divisional manager and of the central agency were the same.
2. That the risk classes of each division and of the parent company are the same. Solomons acknowledges the variations

---

[2] Solomons considered this issue when discussing which cost of capital rate should be used to calculate residual income.

in the riskiness of individual divisions, but he justifies his argument for the use of the company cost of capital as a discount rate at divisional level by claiming that divisional effect on the riskiness of the parent company cannot be assessed by looking at them one at a time. While acknowledging the difficulties involved in attempting to assess the riskiness of individual divisions, Solomons' argument is unconvincing. One effect of the use of a unique discount rate is that divisions with activities involving higher risks and associated higher returns are likely to have greater opportunities for expansion than divisions with activities involving lower risks and lower returns. This may have the effect of making the company as a whole act as if it were a risk-seeker, even if its "real" preference were to make risk-averse decisions.

The use of different divisional discount rates based on the discount rates of similar independent companies is also amenable to criticism, since this could hinder overall company interest. It is unlikely that these different discount rates will reflect the favourable effects (arising from a reduction of risk for the company as a whole) on overall company cost of capital achieved by appropriate corporate diversification; therefore, company investment policy may be far from optimal.

Ma (1969) has suggested using the capitalisation patterns of independent companies similar to those of the company divisions to establish weights for the company's respective costs for each class of capital funds. These weights would then be applied to the overall cost of capital of the parent company to generate a weighted average cost that could be used as the divisional discount rate. Although this suggestion removes some of the limitations of the above two approaches, the weights used may be determined arbitrarily, and this could upset the optimal investment policy of the company.

In recognition of the above difficulties, Shwayder (1970) has advocated the use of a default-free imputed interest rate and letting the users of divisional financial statements apply their own individual risk classes to the risk-free calculations. There does not, thus, appear to be a generally accepted solution for the discount rate problem. Below, we explore further the possibility of deriving divisional specific cost of capital figures using capital asset pricing theory.

DERIVING DIVISIONAL RISK PREMIUMS

Divisional systematic risk

The measurement of risk for a division of a company is not a straightforward matter, given that divisions typically have no shares traded on the stock market. To cope with this difficulty, some writers have suggested adapting the capital asset pricing model (CAPM), extensively used in the finance literature, to provide estimates of risk for untraded securities, such as divisions (e.g. Gordon and Halpern, 1974; Ezzamel, 1979; Fuller and Kerr, 1981).[3] This adaptation is based on the contention that some accounting variables, which are available for company sub-units, can proxy adequately the unobtainable market variables, and hence good estimates of divisional systematic risk can be derived. It is well established that the risk-adjusted discount rate is made of two components: a risk-free component and a risk premium. Hence, the risk-adjusted discount rate, k_t^j, can be expressed as:

$$k_t^j = R_f + \varnothing_t^j \tag{3.14}$$

R_f is the risk-free return as before, and $\varnothing_t^j$ is the appropriate divisional risk premium, so that for divisions with different risk classes $k_t^1 \neq k_t^2 \neq \ldots \neq k_t^m$.

According to the CAPM developed by Sharpe (1964), Lintner (1965) and Mossin (1969), the expected return on an asset or on division j has two elements, which correspond to those in equation (3.14); that is the risk-free return and a risk premium which is the product of the number of units of risk involved and the market price per unit of risk. This is typically expressed as:

---

[3] This discussion is largely based on Ezzamel (1979).

$$E(R_t^j) = R_f + \frac{[E(R_t^m) - R_f]\,\sigma_{jm}}{\sigma^2_m} \qquad (3.15)$$

where:

$E(R_t^j)$ =   the expected return on division j in period t

R_f =   the riskless interest rate

$E(R_t^m)$ =   the expected return on market portfolio in period t

σ^2_m =   the variance of $E(R_t^m)$

σ_{jm} =   the covariance between R_t^j and R_t^m .

In equation (3.15) the quantity of risk carried by division j is σ_{jm}/σ^2_m (that is the division's beta, or the covariance of its returns with the market portfolio scaled down by the market risk) and the price per unit of risk is $[E(R_t^m) - R_f]$, which is the excess of the return on the market portfolio over the risk-free return.

But $K_t^j = E(R_t^j)$, and by comparing equations (3.14) and (3.15) we notice that the first term on the right-hand side of each equation is the same, and $ø_t^j = \{[E(R_t^m) - R_f]/\sigma^2_m\}\,\sigma_{jm}$. Writing $\beta_t^j = \sigma_{jm}/\sigma^2_m$ and substituting for $ø_t^j$ in (3.14) we have:

$$K_t^j = R_f + \beta_t^j\,[E(R_t^m) - R_f] \qquad (3.14a)$$

The risk premium in the risk-adjusted divisional cost of capital is therefore:

$$K_t^j - R_f = \beta_t^j\,[E\,(R_t^m) - R_f] \qquad (3.16)$$

Equation (3.16) shows that the risk premium for division j is proportional to its β^j, with β^j in turn being proportional to σ_{jm}, since σ^2_m will be the same for all assets. This seems to be reasonable, since σ_{jm} reflects the contribution of division j to the variance of the return on the market portfolio, and also the market portfolio is assumed to be the only stochastic component in all efficient portfolios. Part A of Appendix 3.1 examines a conceptual problem with the above model which turns out to be less critical from a practical point of view.

Having derived the theoretical model, the next step is to proxy the unavailable market-based data input into that model. What is needed, therefore, is some accounting-based variable, for example net income (this and similar variables are discussed in more detail below), which is highly correlated with market-based risk. One means of doing this would be to construct a market portfolio using some "suitable" accounting variable for a large sample of firms, and to calculate the covariance between the corresponding variable for a given division and the markets portfolio, $\sigma_{j,m}$ (see Appendix 3.1, part B). This would provide an accounting-based measure of risk for each division which is analogous, but not identical, to the conventional market-based measure of systematic risk. These estimates could be further made to correspond more closely to market-based betas by adjusting them in proportion to the parent company's market-based beta divided by the parent company's accounting-based beta (see equation (3.23) in Appendix 3.1).

Once the beta (or systematic risk) for each division is calculated in the above manner, it becomes possible to derive the divisional cost of capital, $\hat{K}_t^j$, by substituting accounting-based beta, $\hat{\beta}_t^j$, for market-based beta, β_t^j in equation (3.14a) as follows:

$$\hat{K}_t^j = R_f + \hat{\beta}_t^j \left[E(R_t^m) - R_f \right] \tag{3.17}$$

Alternative candidates for estimating divisional systematic risk

Many writers have suggested using accounting numbers as a basis for estimating the systematic risk, β, of a firm.[4] The results of some empirical studies have increased the credibility of this contention; these studies have shown that it is possible to derive accounting-determined measures of risk which closely approximate market risk. Brown and Ball (1967) used the levels of six earnings variables to estimate systematic risk: net income, operating income, net income plus after-tax interest expense, adjusted earnings per share (EPS), operating income/total assets, and net income plus

---

[4] Some may suggest using $\hat{\beta}$ of traded firm J that is similar in every respect to division j as a proxy for β^j, such that $\hat{\beta}^j \cong \beta^j$. This, in a way, is similar to the Modigliani-Miller risk class argument. Various empirical studies have challenged the existence of such equivalent risk classes – see, for example, Gonedes (1969).

after-tax interest expense/total assets. Ball and Brown (1969) used the first differences in earnings (change in firm's earnings) to provide estimates of systematic risk. Both studies suggest that the above accounting income variables appear to predict systematic risk moderately well. With the exception of EPS, each of these variables can be used to derive estimates of systematic risk for company divisions, β^j.

Beaver, Kettler and Scholes (1970) tested the degree of association between seven accounting-determined risk measures and market-determined risk. Of these seven accounting measures, three are relevant to non-traded divisions: average asset growth, average asset size and average liquidity – each is available in traditional accounting statements.

Gordon and Halpern (1974) have suggested using the rate of growth in earnings, instead of the levels of earnings or the first differences in earnings that were used in the earlier studies, as a superior basis to provide a surrogate for divisional systematic risk. They estimate the slope of the regression line, $\hat{\rho}_t^j$ – see Appendix 3.1, equation (3.20) – using the regression:

$$g_t^j = \hat{\alpha}^j + \hat{\rho}_t^j \, g_t^m \tag{3.18}$$

where:

g_t^j = the rate of growth of earnings for division j in period t
g_t^m = the rate of growth of earnings of the market portfolio in period t.

In (3.18) above, g_t^j can be based either on divisional operating income or on divisional net income. Gordon and Halpern argue that β^j and $\hat{\rho}^j$ derived as in (3.18) are likely to be highly correlated. Their argument is based on the assumption that if an entity's earnings grow at a constant rate over time, its share price and dividend will grow at the same rate, provided that some restrictive conditions are satisfied.[5]

---

[5] These conditions are:
  (a) The yield investors require on shares, K_t^A, does not change over time such that $K_1^A = K_2^A = \ldots. = K_N^A = K^A$.
  (b) All earnings are paid in dividends.
  (c) The actual value of earnings at the beginning of the period is the expected earnings in every future period, i.e. myopic revision of expectations.

The above empirical studies show that there are many accounting instrumental variables, i.e. non-market data, that can be used to provide estimates of divisional systematic risk, $\hat{\beta}^j$. The practice by many American and British companies of providing published information about divisional turnover, assets and earnings is very helpful in this respect. However, there are at least two points that can be raised against the divisional cost of capital model suggested above. First, we argued in the previous chapter that accounting income indices are, generally, inappropriate for monitoring divisional performance, yet we suggest a cost of capital model that is based on some accounting income numbers. The response to this criticism is that accounting instrumental variables will only be used as statistical estimators, and not as performance indices *per se*. An "unreliable" performance index could be a "good" statistical estimator; this, we argue, could be the case with accounting income numbers.[6]

Second, implicit in the cost of capital model advocated above is the use of *ex-post* data to provide estimates of $\hat{\beta}^j$ that then will be used as a basis for *ex-ante* decisions. Some empirical evidence, particularly the study by Joyce and Vogel (1970), suggests that the variance, as a measure of risk, calculated using available *ex-post* data is ambiguous and yields conflicting results: this consequently suggests that $\hat{\beta}^j$ will have similar limitations. The problem here seems to be related to the period over which the variance is calculated. The above authors found that there was more than one variance associated with each series of share prices, depending upon the time span considered. This, it seems, is a typical anomaly that can be handled using standard econometric techniques which deal with data bias.

Clearly, these and other arguments against the use of DCF need to be carefully assessed and contrasted with arguments for DCF.

---

[6] If the extent of divisional interdependence is substantial (e.g. where arbitrary transfer prices are used and the volume of internal transfers is significant), the reliability of divisional income as a statistical estimator may be questionable.

SUMMARY

In this chapter attention was focused on providing a detailed examination of the concepts and techniques underlying the use of DCF-based measures of divisional performance. Initially, DCF performance measures were derived in a world of certainty; these were later revised to take account of uncertainty. Alternative ways of incorporating DCF-based divisional targets into a divisional goal model were considered. The main focus there was on the extent of trade off between short-term performance, as reflected in actual cash flows at the end of a particular period, and long-term performance, as reflected in projected cash flows over future years. It was stated there that, given uncertainty over future cash flow projections as well as discount rates but at the same time given the desire to emphasise long-term performance, the choice is quite problematic.

This was followed by a discussion of some of the challenges to DCF applications. These included the extent of reliability of cash flow forecasts and the implications of that for performance evaluation, the unclear relationship between recovered depreciation equivalent and physical depreciation of assets and the difficulty of income attribution to specific short-term periods (e.g. one year). The most challenging problem, however, is that related to the determination of the discount rate, both in terms of time preference and risk premium. We have suggested that the discount rate should reflect differences in divisional risk classes, rather than be the same for all divisions. A procedure for making divisional discount rates responsive to variations in divisional riskiness was developed. The procedure relies on the use of the basic capital asset pricing model where divisional accounting parameters replace the conventional market parameters to generate divisional accounting-related betas. Various accounting variables were examined in order to identify those that are most suitable for the purposes of deriving divisional betas.

Notwithstanding the powerful theoretical arguments in support of DCF-based divisional income measures, empirical evidence indicates that such measures are hardly, if ever, embraced by practitioners. Those who make use of DCF-based measures also tend in the main to use conventional measures. In this latter case it is not entirely clear how much importance is attached to DCF-based measures *vis-à-vis* conventional measures; however, given the widespread scepticism which practitioners have shown regarding the use of difficult-to-apply techniques, it will not be surprising if they subordinate DCF measures to conventional measures. Given this schism between theory and practice, it is legitimate to question whether continued efforts to sharpen and develop DCF techniques are worthwhile. Instead of resorting to extreme arguments, it is more helpful to make a double appeal:

1. An appeal to academics to root their research relating to DCF techniques in practice as far as possible, rather than to engage in research that is deemed to be only of academic interest.

2. An appeal to practitioners to show more readiness to experiment with non-conventional techniques such as DCF, and to pioneer initiatives which bring them closer to academics, in an attempt to work jointly on issues of common interest.

The analyses in Chapters 2 and 3 focused in the main on using financial measures to guide and monitor operating decisions. In the following chapter we extend the analysis to non-recurrent, capital investment decisions.

APPENDIX 3.1

(A) The problem is mainly conceptual; Fama (1968) has shown that the risk premium derived according to equation (3.16) is incorrect. This is because the equation is based on the inconsistent assumptions of Sharpe's diagonal model.[7] Fama derives an alternative risk premium of the form:

---

[7] In Sharpe's diagonal model the return on asset i is given by:
$$R_i = \alpha_i + \beta_i R^m + \epsilon_i$$
Where α_i and β_i are parameters associated with asset i and ϵ_i is a disturbance element with the properties: $E(\epsilon_i) = 0$, $\sigma_{\epsilon_i, \epsilon_j} = 0$, and $\sigma_{\epsilon_{i,m}} = 0$. However:

$$R^m = \sum_{i=1}^{N} W_i R_i = \sum_{i=1}^{N} W_i [\alpha_i + \beta_i R^m + \epsilon_i]$$

Since ϵ_i is part of R_m, the condition $\sigma_{\epsilon_{i,m}} = 0$ is inconsistent.

$$K_i^j - R_f = \theta_t \left\{ \beta^j \sum_{i=1}^{N} W^i \beta^i \sigma^2 (r_m) + W^j \sigma^2 (\epsilon^j) \right\} \quad (3.19)$$

where:

$$\theta_t = [E(R_t^m) - R_f]/\sigma^2_m ,$$

r_m = common underlying market factor which affects the returns on all assets such that:

$$R^i = \alpha^i + \beta^i r_m + \epsilon^i, i = 1,2 \ldots, N, \text{ and}$$
$$R^m = \sum_{i=1}^{N} W^i R^i = \sum_{i=1}^{N} W^i [\alpha^i + \beta^i r_m + \epsilon^i]$$

with $E(\epsilon^i) = 0$, $\sigma_{\epsilon i, \epsilon j} = 0$, and $\sigma_{\epsilon, im} = 0$, W^j = the proportion of the total value of all assets accounted for by division j. However, as Fama has pointed out, from a practical viewpoint expressions (3.16) and (3.19) are nearly equal. Hence, despite the technical limitations of (3.16) indicated above, it can still be used as a good proxy for the risk equivalent of a division.

(B) Assume that some set of "non-market" statistic, n_t^j, which is applicable to both "traded" and "non-traded" firms, exists. Each of these statistics can be used to derive $\hat{\rho}^j$ for any j division using the regression:

$$n_{it}^j = \alpha_{it}^j + \hat{\rho}_{it}^j n_{it}^m \quad (3.20)$$

where:

n_{it}^j represents the "non-market" statistic i for division j in period t;

n_{it}^m represents the "non-market" statistic i for the market portfolio in period t;

$\alpha_{it}^j, \hat{\rho}_{it}^j$ represents the intercept and the slope of the regression line.

The $\bar{\hat{\rho}}_i^j$ with the highest correlation coefficient with $\hat{\beta}^j$, $\hat{\rho}_i^j$, can then be used as a proxy for divisional systematic risk. But $\hat{\beta}^j$ can only be derived for "traded" firms; hence $\bar{\hat{\rho}}_i^j$ can be correlated with $\hat{\beta}^j$ for "traded" firms, and the resulting coefficient can be assumed to hold for "non-traded" divisions. Therefore, for "traded" firms we have:

$$\hat{\beta}_t^j = \lambda_0 + \lambda_1 \, \bar{\rho}_t^j \qquad (3.21)$$

where $\bar{\rho}^j$ is the "non-market"-based divisional systematic risk with the highest correlation coefficient with $\hat{\beta}^j$. In fact, a more "meaningful" expression for $\hat{\beta}^j$ is of the form:

$$\hat{\beta}_t^j = \lambda_0 + \lambda_1 \hat{\rho}_{1t}^j + \lambda_2 \hat{\rho}_{2t}^j + \ldots + \lambda_s \hat{\rho}_{st}^j = \lambda_0 + \sum_{i=1}^{s} \lambda_i \hat{\rho}_{it}^j \qquad (3.22)$$

Although one would expect that the $\hat{\rho}_i^j$'s are correlated together, a multiple regression form similar to that in (3.22) is likely to provide a smaller residual error than the simple regression form expressed in (3.21). The values of the λ_i's derived for a "traded" firm can then be used as relative weights in calculating the systematic risk for "non-traded" divisions.

We need to investigate further the relationship between $\bar{\rho}^j$ and $\hat{\beta}^j$ in (3.21) or the $\hat{\rho}^j$'s and $\hat{\beta}^j$ in (3.22); for simplicity we concentrate on (3.21). The usefulness of (3.21) as a basis for deriving divisional cost of capital depends on the extent to which $\hat{\rho}^j$ approximates $\hat{\beta}^j$. Ideally, $\lambda_0 = 0$ and $\lambda_1 = 1$ in (3.21), such that $\hat{\beta}^j = \bar{\rho}^j$. But since $\hat{\beta}^j$ is based on market data while $\hat{\rho}^j$ is derived using "non-market" data, it is likely that $\hat{\beta}^j \neq \bar{\rho}^j$.

Assume now that for each of two "traded" firms A and j $\hat{\beta}^A \neq \bar{\rho}^A$ and $\hat{\beta}^j \neq \bar{\rho}^j$ respectively. For the two firms, $\hat{\beta}^A$ and $\hat{\beta}^j$ can be derived directly from (3.14a). However, if $\lfloor \hat{\beta}^j/\hat{\beta}^A \rfloor = \lfloor \bar{\rho}^j/\bar{\rho}^A \rfloor$, $\hat{\beta}^j$ can be derived indirectly from $\hat{\beta}^A$ if data relating to the latter term were available as follows:

$$\hat{\beta}_t^j = \hat{\beta}_t^A \frac{\bar{\rho}_t^j}{\bar{\rho}_t^A} \qquad (3.23)$$

The above reasoning can be extended to the case of a "non-traded" division if the following conditions hold:

1. The securities of the parent company are traded on the market.

2. Equation (3.20) applies to both "traded" and "non-traded" firms.
3. The relationship $\lfloor \hat{\beta}^j/\hat{\beta}^A \rfloor = \lfloor \bar{\hat{\rho}}^j/\bar{\hat{\rho}}^A \rfloor$ holds for division j if securities were traded on the market.

In (3.23) above, $\hat{\beta}^A$ can be obtained from the capital asset pricing model according to condition (1) – see equation (3.14a). Also, $\bar{\hat{\rho}}^j$ and $\bar{\hat{\rho}}^A$ can be estimated by means of regression (3.22) according to condition (2). Hence, if the above conditions hold it will be possible to derive the cost of capital for a "non-traded" division that would obtain if the securities of the division were traded on the market such that:

$$\hat{K}_t^j = R_f + \hat{\beta}_t^j [E(R_t^m) - R_f] \qquad (3.24)$$

If condition (3) above does not hold, $\hat{\beta}^j$ derived according to (3.23) and $\hat{K}^j$ derived according to (3.24) will not, in general, correspond to $\hat{\beta}^j$ and $\hat{K}^j$ which would be obtained if the securities of the division were traded on the market. Despite this limitation, it would be more plausible to use $\hat{\beta}^j$ derived according to (3.23) as a proxy for divisional systematic risk than to rely entirely on $\bar{\hat{\rho}}^j$.

QUESTIONS

1. Outline and evaluate the basic assumptions of the discounted cash flow concept of income.
2. The financial director of Dimax Ltd, a divisionalised company making and selling a wide-ranging product line in electronics, has asked you, as her special advisor, to offer advice in relation to improving the company's performance evaluation system which currently evaluates divisional performance on the basis of accounting profit. The financial director has recently been on a course on financial management, organised by one of the leading universities, in which she was introduced to the concept of discounted cash flow (DCF). She is now seriously considering the possibility of formulating divisional targets using DCF and seeks your help in exploring alternative ways

for developing divisional goal models based on DCF. Prepare a report containing the alternatives you propose, and comment on the suitability of each alternative for the purposes of divisional performance measurement.

3. Explain and evaluate the main challenges to the application of DCF techniques in the context of evaluating divisional performance.

4. Explore the possibility of developing estimates of divisional cost of capital utilising some of the findings of the capital asset pricing model. Which set of accounting variables can be usefully used to proxy market returns? What are the advantages and limitations of using such divisional cost of capital estimates to determine divisional DCF income targets?

4

Monitoring Divisional Capital Investment Decisions

The main focus of the analysis in the preceding chapters has been on monitoring divisional performance with respect to operating decisions. Underlying that analysis, however, was the important notion of motivating divisional managers to make optimal investment decisions, since the level of operating activities is determined ultimately by the level of capital resources utilised by a particular division. Thus, in contrasting accounting profit, ROI, residual income and DCF as measures of business unit and divisional performance, a main question that was posed was: which of these indices yields and secures optimal sub-unit investment levels? Similarly, in assessing the overall suitability of each of these indices for the purposes of divisional performance measurement we documented several instances in which sub-optimal capital budgeting decisions are likely to occur. For example, it was suggested that when ROI calculations are based on the net book value of assets, the purchase of new and more long-term economic equipment may be delayed to avoid increasing the investment base which would, *ceteris paribus*, result in a lower ROI (see Chapter 2). It is clear then that divisional capital budgeting decisions have a crucial effect on divisional and, by implication, corporate performance.

In order to provide a more complete analysis of business unit and divisional performance, in this chapter we focus more explicitly on the concepts, processes and techniques which can be deployed to monitor capital budgeting decisions in divisionalised organisations. First, we discuss the theoretical framework for capital investment decisions advanced in the literature on divisionalisation. Next, we examine some of the available evidence on corporate practices drawn from in-depth business history studies and from questionnaire-based research. This is followed by a description of a formal model of capital resource allocation in organisations and a summary of DCF-based evaluation techniques. Finally, the last section contains a summary of the chapter.

THE THEORETICAL FRAMEWORK

Williamson's (1970; 1975) work on markets and hierarchies offers a framework in which the M-form organisation is postulated to operate as a miniature capital market. The special attributes of the M-form are assumed to endow it with greater efficiency, compared with external capital markets. This framework sets the scene for the organisation of financing and investment decisions within the divisionalised firm. Further, in establishing the argument for the superiority, in terms of economic efficiency, of the M-form over the centralised U-form, Williamson includes as a basic ingredient of the control apparatus of the M-form a resource allocation system which is assumed to be especially suited to the divisionalised firm. This system reallocates cash flows generated by individual divisions to high-yield projects, after soliciting investment proposals from the divisions and evaluating them on a corporate-wide basis, rather than merely allowing cash flows to revert back to the divisions from which they originated.

The theoretical framework developed by Williamson is related to competition in the capital market. His analysis commences by alluding to the problems caused by the separation of ownership from control in U-form organisations. Although the U-form made possible the realisation of economies of scale, increase in size and complexity led to the separation of ownership from control, with potentially adverse consequences for performance. The administrative integration of various functions, which occurs in U-form firms, can impair the capital market's monitoring capabilities.

Williamson contends that the M-form overcomes these problems because it is able to operate as a miniature capital market, with superior attributes of economic efficiency compared with external capital markets. The monitoring capabilities of the external capital market are impaired for three reasons: as an external monitor it cannot always secure firm-specific information relevant to monitoring; it can only perform non-marginal adjustments resulting in major rewards or sanctions; and it is a costly monitoring device. By contrast, the M-form internal capital market has several distinct advantages. First, it is an internal monitoring mechanism with the requisite authority and expertise to obtain information relevant for contemporaneous evaluations of the operating efficiency of each division. Second, through its access to an elaborate reward system, it can engineer marginal and non-marginal adjustments, ranging from minor financial rewards and sanctions to major promotions/demotions and dismissal of managers. Third, it can perform intervention at a relatively low cost. This last advantage, i.e. economy of internal communication and intervention, makes it possible within an M-form firm for the internal investment process to be decomposed into various stages in a sequential manner.

This would allow for additional financing of investment proposals to be conditional on prior stage results and emerging contingencies. Such sequential, and evidently useful, decision-making process would be extremely costly in the context of external capital markets. For Williamson (1970, pp. 140–1):

> The M-form organization can thus be viewed as capitalism's creative response to the evident limit which the capital market experiences in its relations to the firm as well as a means for overcoming the organizational problems which develop in the large U-form enterprise when variety becomes great . . .. The realization of

operating economies by reconstituting a large U-form enterprise along M-form lines represents a source of potential profit gain which, in the absence of reorganization, is unavailable. The resulting economies are due to more effective resource allocation (between divisions and in the aggregate), better internal organization (a reduction in the technical control loss), and the attenuation of sub-goal pursuit.

Williamson (1975) contends further that the superiority of the M-form firm as a miniature capital market goes beyond the attenuation of managerial opportunistic behaviour, as divisional managers may be encouraged to take risks which would be declined if the division was a stand-alone firm. This is because managers of independent firms, realising that performance evaluation focuses on the outcomes of their actions rather than the decision processes, will have a vested interest in engaging in low-risk activities. In an M-form firm, Williamson argues, managers will be motivated to be more aggressive risk-takers because the multidivisional form allows them low-cost access to a wide range of elaborate decision-making techniques.

The conglomerate (i.e. horizontal merger) form of organisation is of immediate relevance to the arguments underpinning Williamson's framework. The conventional literature has been dismissive of any significant potential economies of synergy that could be attributed to conglomerates, with whatever minimal gains obtainable accruing mainly from risk-pooling and operating economies. Williamson examines these arguments further by focusing on the question of whether risk-pooling adequately reflects the investment advantages and operating efficiency properties of M-form firms with conglomerate characteristics. In a divisionalised non-conglomerate firm, funds earmarked for specific investments could merely represent delayed responses to market signals, or be simply the outcome of arbitrary allocation procedures. By contrast, in a conglomerate, cash flows generated from diverse internal sources are not automatically retained by the divisions which generated them, but are pooled centrally and then allocated rationally on the basis of expected future returns. As Williamson (1970, p. 143) points out:

> The conglomerate acts in this respect as a miniature capital market;
> it internalizes the funds metering function normally imputed to the

capital market – a function which Baumol's analysis of the traditional mechanisms found to be defective.

Related to this discussion is the diversification argument attributed to the conglomerate firm. Being an amalgam of diverse, highly unrelated, horizontally integrated businesses, the conglomerate firm offers obvious diversification advantages in the context of reducing the overall risk of the firm. But as Williamson has pointed out, the diversification argument is subject to diminishing returns. For a given size of firm, increasing the extent of diversification leads to increased complexity and hence results in diminution of control. Achieving optimal diversification requires that operating efficiency for given size and investment alternatives be finely balanced. Conversely, as the extent of diversification increases while holding the firm size constant, variety becomes more difficult to manage, given fixed hierarchical arrangements.

However, the conglomerate form has its limitations; in particular it can trigger serious antitrust implications through mega–merger activities, and it has not yet been established beyond reasonable doubt that its diversification achievements are either cheaper or even necessary for individual investors, given the latter's ability to diversify risks fairly cheaply.

It is clear from the preceding discussion that investment decisions are an integral part of the argument for M-form firms. Indeed, Williamson (1975, p. 148) has gone to the extent of suggesting that the "assignment of cash flows to high yield uses is the most fundamental attribute of the M-form enterprise." Because of this critical importance, the investment process has to be carefully monitored. Williamson (1970) distinguishes between three different types of investment monitoring, all of which are deemed necessary for rational investment decisions; advance, contemporaneous, and *ex post*.

Advance evaluation entails reviewing investment proposals involving criteria related to the intrinsic merits of these proposals, the balance between the different parts, and the level of expenditure. Such advanced monitoring helps in linking investment decisions more closely to corporate strategy and to organisational objectives. It also provides managers with the incentive of tuning their investment proposals not only to divisional interests but also to corporate-wide interests.

Contemporaneous monitoring involves comparing current performance against targets, identifying variances and examining their sources, and contrasting performance with that of major competitors. This is "on-the-spot" control, based on regular and timely observation, feedback and intervention, so that potential future variances can be avoided.

Finally, *ex-post* monitoring takes the form of repeated comparisons of actual results against targets, identification of variances and then examination of their causes. Unlike the previous two types of monitoring, the role of *ex-post* monitoring is not instant correction but rather building up a useful database that can be used to determine managerial efficiency, improving future target setting, and redirecting future cash flows to more efficient divisions.

These audit procedures are likely to be executed more effectively in an M-form firm compared with the external capital market. As divisional managers are subordinates, their accounting records and files are easily accessed by central management for monitoring purposes, whereas investors (particularly shareholders) would not be guaranteed such unlimited access. Further, cooperation in terms of disclosure of sensitive information is likely to be secured within an M-form firm, as members are all internal to one organisation, compared with the external capital market, where outsiders are involved.

RESOURCE ALLOCATION: EMPIRICAL EVIDENCE

The previous section outlined the skeletal theoretical framework for resource allocation in divisionalised organisations, as developed mainly by Williamson. This section seeks to provide some empirical evidence relating to resource allocation practices in these organisations. The evidence is drawn from two different, but complementary, literature sources; historical and case study.

Historical evidence

The historical evidence on resource allocation practices is based on a few in-depth studies of specific organisations, as documented by writers such as Sloan (1963), Chandler (1962; 1977), Johnson (1978) and Chandler and Daems (1979).

Chandler (1977) and Chandler and Daems (1979) have documented how, towards the end of the nineteenth century, the modern hierarchical firm, among other functions, internalised resource allocation, thereby supplanting the market and the price system. Increased cash flow resulting from greater economies of speed and economies of scale led to the accumulation of larger amounts of internally generated funds which could be utilised in making new investments. Such growth in internal funding, coupled with increased competition for funds among operating units, led to the internalisation of resource allocation by firms. Pioneering firms began to develop capital appropriation schemes which ranged from those that were crude, as in the case of Standard Oil, to those that were highly elaborate and systematic, as in the case of Du Pont and General Motors.

At Du Pont, capital appropriation procedures were developed which emphasised the use of carefully projected rates of return and precise rules to obtain approval for proposed appropriations. Monthly forecasts of the company's future financial position were used to determine the maximum amount which could be invested in new projects from retained earnings. Careful scrutiny of relative project profitability on a company-wide basis was undertaken so that "there would be no expenditures for additions to earning equipment if the same amount of money could be applied to some better purpose in another branch of the company's business" (cited in Chandler, 1977, p. 449). Projected rates of return of proposed investment projects were also carefully checked by the sales and traffic (transportation) departments to ensure that the greatest comparative advantage had been secured in the design of proposed facilities and in relation to their location *vis-à-vis* markets, supplies and transportation. As Chandler (1977) has pointed out, such information flow and monitoring arrangements enhanced the possibilities of rational choice being exercised between alternative investment and financing decisions.

Sloan (1963) gives a good account of appropriations of capital spending at General Motors in the 1920s. The system allowed for small amounts of expenditure to be authorised by the divisional manager on his own. In the case of larger amounts, the evaluation of proposed projects rested on four criteria. These were (a) the necessity of the project as a commercial venture; (b) the state of technical development of the project; (c) the appropriateness of the project from the corporate point of view; and (d) the relative value of the project to the corporation, compared with alternative projects, in terms of both profitability and relevance to corporate operation. An Appropriations Committee reviewed all divisional requests of funding before they were submitted to the Executive Committee or Finance Committee for policy review and approval. An appropriations manual was established, detailing the types of information which divisions were requested to present to support proposed expenditures. As Sloan (1963, p. 121) points out:

> The divisions were to make monthly reports of construction in progress to the Appropriations Committee, which in turn would present a combined report each month to the Finance Committee. Each appropriation request was to receive consideration and analysis from a corporation as well as a divisional standpoint before any commitment was made. Proper records were to be kept of expenditures and approvals from expenditures, and uniform treatment was to be given to appropriation requests throughout the corporation.

Forecasts and price indices for each division and for the company as a whole were reviewed by the financial staff of the general office. Further, under the divisionalised structure pioneered by General Motors, general executives were relieved from day-to-day operating decisions. With the help of financial and advisory staff they were able to devote more attention to resource allocation on the basis of divisional performance evaluations, sophisticated forecasts, and detailed capital budgets provided by both the divisions and the advisory staff.

This fully developed resource allocation system contributed to the success of General Motors. By relying on uniform performance criteria in allocating resources to divisions, and by linking managerial compensation to these criteria, in Johnson's words (1978, p. 494) the system "simultaneously encouraged a high degree of automatic compliance with company-wide financial goals and greatly increased the division manager's decentralized autonomy."

According to Johnson, two characteristics of the resource allocation system at General Motors contributed to these achievements. First, the annual forecast was based on plans for expansion which were determined through close collaboration between division managers and top management, which minimised divisional bias in these plans. The expansion plans also effectively placed a lower bound on the planned investment of each divisional manager, thereby acting as a disincentive for managers to forgo investment opportunities which reduced their return on investment whilst being profitable on a company-wide basis. Second, the company's financial reporting system emphasised capital turnover ratios and thus promoted initiative and ingenuity in improving these ratios. This implies that divisional managers enjoyed substantial autonomy in planning specific investment projects.

A particularly interesting feature of the General Motors resource allocation system was its punitive nature; divisional managers had to comply with corporate policies to avoid possible reductions in their resources. The resource allocation system was therefore 'flexible' in the sense that allocations were not strictly dependent upon differential returns on investment. Further, the allocation system at times assessed divisional managers in terms of differential target rates of return. Yet, there is some evidence of opportunistic behaviour which took place in some of these pioneering companies. Chandler and Daems (1979) have suggested that despite the use of systematic resource allocation schemes, there were frequent occasions in which allocation decisions were determined by negotiations between department heads (divisional managers) which emphasised departmental priorities at the expense of the overall interest of the corporation.

To summarise, the preceding historical evidence demonstrates when, how, and why in-firm hierarchical arrangements supplanted market arrangements as a means of resource allocation. Towards the end of the nineteenth century, pioneering divisionalised organisations such as General Motors possessed, or evolved, the requisite characteristics which helped to decouple them from market-based allocation mechanisms. These characteristics were:

(a) the ability to accumulate large internal funds which could be diverted from dividend payments into investment projects; (b) the availability of rigorous and systematic internal resource allocation schemes which could lead to efficient allocation of resources; and (c) the availability of other monitoring arrangements (e.g. reward schemes, internal audit of proposed investment projects) which helped to keep divisional managers in line with corporate objectives. The resource allocation systems employed in the main uniform criteria for allocations, but they remained sufficiently flexible to take account of special circumstances and were amenable to fine-tuning. As Williamson (1975) has pointed out, external market-based allocation mechanisms are denied such flexibility. Further, the operation of internal resource allocation schemes generates the requisite information at a cheaper cost, compared with external capital markets. This evidence, however, is based on the detailed examination of a few, if large and pioneering, companies. Below, we review some empirical evidence on resource allocation practices drawn from larger samples of American and British companies.

Evidence from questionnaire-based studies

Several questionnaire-based empirical investigations into the nature of the resource allocation process in divisionalised organisations have been undertaken. Overall, the findings suggest that divisional managers have limited measures of autonomy over resource allocation and significant investment decisions. Further, various internal audit and monitoring schemes are employed by firms in order to keep divisional investment decisions in line with corporate interest. There are, however, some indications that these controls are not always operative, with the consequence that divisional managers at times exercise greater power over such crucial decisions than is deemed optimal from the perspective of the markets and hierarchies theory.

As a starting point, it is worth reporting the findings relating to divisional discretion with respect to raising external finance. Here, existing empirical evidence is consistent in suggesting that divisional managers have virtually no autonomy in raising external funds, be they of a long-term or a short-term nature (Baumes, 1961; Tomkins, 1973; Ezzamel and Hilton, 1980b; Scapens and Sale, 1981). This finding is in keeping with the main tenet of the markets and hierarchies theory, since most financing decisions are strategic and since there are strong economy arguments in dealing with external finance matters on a central basis (see also Amey, 1969a). Another relevant finding is that most divisions are obliged to return the cash flows they generate to a central pool of funds, and then subsequently seek funds from the headquarters to finance their proposed capital projects which are evaluated by the centre with the aid of accounting-based or market-based measures (Scapens and Sale, 1981). This is consistent with Williamson's argument of allocating cash flows to high-yield uses determined on a corporate-wide basis as detailed earlier.

In respect of resource allocation for investment purposes, divisional managers appear to fare only marginally better than in the case of raising external finance. Here, all the above studies (see also Schall, Sundem and Geijsbeek, 1978; Pike, 1983) point to divisional managers having little say in specifying the amounts of capital expenditure in their annual budgets. In some cases, particularly when companies were relatively small, the headquarters required divisional managers to obtain formal authorisation for almost all capital expenditures, barring those involving trivial amounts. In most cases, however, divisional managers had to seek authorisation for capital project expenditures above certain limits, which were usually quite low and did not appear to be related to divisional size or to the nature of the project under consideration (Scapens and Sale, 1981). Further, the above studies also indicate that divisional managers have restricted levels of autonomy in respect of choosing capital projects within capital expenditure limits, but that their autonomy is somewhat greater compared with that relating to specifying capital expenditure limits (Ezzamel and Hilton, 1980b). Again, these arguments are consistent with those of Williamson, and indicate a diffusion of the practices of the pioneering divisionalised firms among most contemporary divisionalised companies.

There is also insightful empirical evidence relating to formal pre-decision and post-decision controls of divisional capital investments. The study of Scapens, Sale and Tikkas (1982) suggests that pre-decision controls of divisional capital investments include using long-term corporate plans as a means of communicating investment goals to divisions, issuing broad guidelines to divisions which are expected to produce their own long-term plans, and above all, the direct involvement of corporate headquarters in the preparation of divisional capital expenditure budgets. All these controls aim to motivate divisional managers to pursue investment projects which are consistent with corporate interest. In addition, financial analysis techniques are widely used to evaluate divisional investment proposals which exceed prescribed capital expenditure ceilings, even though many of them are crude and limited in scope, e.g. the pay-back method.

Post-decision controls of divisional capital investment can be indirect, in the form of financial measures used to assess divisional performance, or direct, such as monitoring and auditing implementation of capital investment. Clearly capital investment decisions affect divisional financial performance, particularly if measures of performance are explicitly related to the investment base, as in the case of residual income and return on investment, the use of which is widespread among divisionalised companies. Direct monitoring of implementation of divisional capital investment includes project accounts, which are normally the responsibility of divisional accountants, detailing expenditures incurred on authorised capital projects, and post-completion audits, that is audits of the outcome of capital projects. Post-completion audits involve a variety of mechanisms, ranging from *ad hoc* reviews of specific projects, to regular reviews of the costs and benefits achieved on authorised projects (Scapens, Sale and Tikkas, 1982).

Several researchers, however, have suggested that much of the reported centralisation of decision-making power in the area of divisional investment decisions is more apparent than real. For example, Bower (1970) has reported that the approval by corporate headquarters of divisional investment proposals was in the main a formality among American companies. Morgan and Luck (1973) could not identify any instances in which capital investment proposals were rejected once they had reached the stage of formal application for corporate approval, among British companies, a finding which was corroborated further by Scapens and Sale (1981). Similarly, Pike (1983) observed only a 10 per cent rejection rate of divisional investment proposals among large UK firms, and even lower rejection rates in smaller companies.

Overall, the above suggests that, although divisionalised organisations have evolved several elaborate mechanisms aiming at curtailing the power of divisional managers over investment decisions, in reality divisional managers exert much greater influence over these decisions. Certainly, one of the limitations of many of the existing empirical studies in this area is their focus on formal monitoring mechanisms, to the exclusion of informal measures, and their reduction of the rather complex investment decision process into an apparently simple phenomenon. Bower (1970, pp. 320–1) describes the complexity of the process of resource allocation so succinctly:

> the most striking aspect of the process of resource allocation . . . is the extent to which it is more complex than most managers seem to believe. It bears little resemblance to the simple portfolio management problem described in traditional finance theory. Moreover, the systems created to control the process sometimes appeared irrelevant to the task. They were based on the fallacious belief that top management made important choices in the finance committee when it approved capital investment proposals. In contrast we have found capital investment to be a process of study, bargaining, persuasion and choice spread over many levels of the organization and over long periods of time.

Bower (1970) has provided an insightful scenario of the resource allocation process in American companies. He has observed that project proposals are initiated at lower organisational levels, e.g. departmental or divisional levels. As the proposals progressed up the organisation, they were evaluated by progressively more senior managers as they gained the support of one manager after another. Hence, investment proposals submitted by divisional managers for headquarters approval would generally already have been evaluated and supported by a significant number of senior managers. This makes it unlikely for these proposals to be rejected by headquarters.

Decision-making involves various stages which can be grouped under decision management (generation of proposals and implementation of ratified decisions) and decision control (ratification and monitoring of decisions) (see Fama and Jensen,

1983a; 1983b). Since the management of investment decisions is likely to reside in the hands of divisional managers, they can exert their influence on capital investment at that stage (see King, 1974; Scapens and Sale, 1981, for a similar argument). Further, although decision control is the prerogative of corporate headquarters, divisional managers may have sufficient informal power to bring to bear on the process of investment decisions. Yet, it would be misleading to always infer greater divisional power over resource allocation from the high approval rates of divisional investment proposals. Bower (1970) has documented evidence which suggests that, over time, divisional managers get to know the characteristics of investment proposals which are likely to gain the approval of corporate headquarters and that these are frequently used as guidelines by divisional managers. This suggests a self-selection process which reflects greater measures of built-in controls, rather than greater divisional power.

Having established the theoretical arguments in support of hierarchical resource allocation mechanisms, and discussed the historical precedence and contemporary practices of divisionalised organisations in this connection, we now proceed to describe and evaluate a formal model of resource allocation which seems particularly suitable for these organisations.

A FORMAL MODEL OF RESOURCE ALLOCATION

Most of the formal and analytical resource allocation models which have been developed in the literature on divisionalisation primarily deal with the problem of determining transfer prices for intra-company transfers. Nevertheless, these models can be adapted quite easily to deal with resource allocation in the context of capital investment decisions, by treating funds as a central or shared resource.

Major advances in the construction of these models have been made possible following the development of the decomposition principle by Dantzig and Wolfe (1963). Before then, resource allocation models (e.g. Arrow, 1959; Arrow and Hurwicz, 1960) could result in infinite iterations without guaranteeing convergence to an optimal solution. Rules of thumb had to be invoked to terminate the iterations, with the consequence that obtained solutions were sub-optimal. In contrast, the decomposition principle is an iterative algorithm which yields an optimal solution after a finite number of iterations.

The development of the decomposition principle signalled the emergence of several mathematical models which can accommodate the allocation of central, or shared, resources such as capital investment funds using arbitrary administrative schemes (see Amey, 1969a), but in the main they rely on the use of an internal pricing mechanism to engineer allocations. Two reasons can be advanced for researchers' preference for internal pricing arrangements. First, it is held that divisional managers enjoy relatively greater measures of decision-making autonomy under the pricing mechanism compared with administrative allocations. Second, unlike other models based on administrative allocation models, decomposition models based on internal pricing guarantee optimal allocations (Amey, 1969a).

A generalised goal decomposition (GGD) model

In this section, we describe a resource allocation model developed by Ruefli (1971a; 1971b) and extended by Bailey and Boe (1976). Compared with other models, this model can incorporate various organisational and behavioural attributes which are particularly relevant to divisionalised organisations.

The GGD model makes use of the decomposition principle and has been developed to deal with resource allocation in decentralised organisations. Like all decomposition models, the GGD model is based on the notion that various organisational sub-units, such as divisions, generate alternative proposals for corporate headquarters in response to prices announced by headquarters. Appropriately adapted (see Bailey and Boe, 1976), the model invokes a tri-level divisionalised organisation consisting of corporate management (CM), divisional management (DM), and operating management (OM). In the context of a planned programmed budgeting system (PPBS), we may interpret CM as a project coordinator, DM as divisions needed to contribute to the project, and OM as the operating units within each division necessary to implement specific operating procedures.

Table 4.1 details the responsibilities of each of the three hierarchical levels in order for the model to operate. Corporate management deals with corporate-level matters which are of major strategic importance: determining organisational goals and also determining the role that each division manager should play in order for divisions to achieve these goals. Divisional management deals with matters strictly relevant to its own division. Thus, given divisional goals, divisional management determines the manner in which resources can be mobilised to achieve these goals; determines the relative priorities of its set of goals; takes steps to keep deviations from goals to a minimum; and determines the objectives that each of its operating units must pursue in order for divisional goals to be achieved. Finally, operating unit management determines the production factors needed for its own activities, given the goals identified for it by divisional management, and takes the necessary steps to minimise its cost targets, by determining the materials and other resources necessary

TABLE 4.1 Responsibilities of hierarchical levels in the GGD model

Hierarchical level	Responsibilities
I. CORPORATE MANAGEMENT (CM):	1. Determine organisational goals. 2. Determine the role of each division in meeting these goals.
II. DIVISIONAL MANAGEMENT (DM):	1. Determine how resources can be used to achieve own goals. 2. Determine priorities of own goals. 3. Minimise deviations from own goals. 4. Determine the objectives of each of its operating units (cost targets).
III. OPERATING UNIT MANAGEMENT (OM):	1. Determine production factors needed for its own activities. 2. Aim to minimise cost target given by division.

for its activities. The operating unit therefore typically focuses its attention on inputs and hence on cost performance, in contrast to the division which will typically be responsible for both inputs and outputs, and hence its goals will reflect some profit target. And just as Williamson (1970; 1975) and others have recommended, corporate management deals with major strategic issues, whilst operating decisions are delegated to the lower divisional management and operating unit levels. The separation of strategic decisions from operating decisions is therefore promoted under this model.

The operation of the GGD model follows a set of steps similar to those of other decomposition models, as illustrated in Figure 4.1. The process starts with each division solving its own problem, specified in terms of minimising positive and negative deviations from its goals, subject to its own constraints and the priorities and prices determined by corporate management, and submitting its dual values for each corporate goal to the CM. The CM then solves its own programme which seeks to maximise corporate profits subject to certain constraints, generating new goal values which are then transmitted to divisional managers for the second iteration. Before the second iteration begins, each division transmits all its dual values, including those relating to divisional resources, to each of its operating units. Each operating unit solves its own programme, and submits the activity levels obtained to its division. The second iteration starts only after all operating units have submitted their new activity levels to their respective divisions. Iterations continue until the programme converges to a solution which is guaranteed by the properties of the algorithm (Ruefli, 1971a). The algorithm of the GGD model is detailed in Appendix 4.1.

The solution to the complete problem is dependent upon the determination of shadow prices for divisional goals. Two sets of shadow prices, or dual values are generated. The first, $\Pi_{k\,f}$ in Appendix 4.1, are the marginal values of the divisional goals at the divisional level, but *relative to corporate goals*. The second set of shadow prices, $\Pi_{k\,r}$ in Appendix 4.1, are the marginal values of the divisional goals at the divisional level *relative to that division's goals*, i.e. those not shared by other divisions or by corporate management. These latter dual values are submitted to the CM

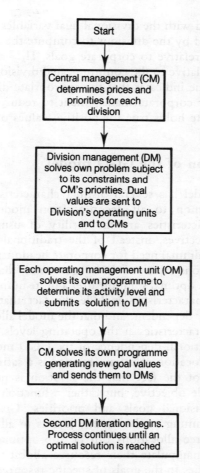

FIGURE 4.1 The operation of the GGD model.

only when divisional goals are included in a later revision of the corporate management model.

Although the GGD model converges to an optimal (satisficing) solution, corporate and divisional problems have differing constraints and as such may lead to different solutions. Thus during the intermediate planning stages the corporate determined goal levels associated with the divisional dual variables will be different from those used by the divisions to compute the dual values. The shadow prices relative to corporate goals, $\Pi_{k\,f}$, are bid prices by the divisions relative to the communicated division goal structure. A negative value indicates that the appropriate division considers it beneficial for corporate management to reduce that goal level, and the opposite holds true for positive values of $\Pi_{k\,f}$.

An evaluation of the GGD model

The GGD model has several distinct characteristics, in addition to those common to all decomposition models. Among the common characteristics are the facility of using multiple and competing objectives, instead of the traditional single objective criterion; the minimal need for corporate headquarters to be aware of divisional constraints; and the guarantee that the algorithm converges to an optimal solution after a finite number of iterations. The distinct characteristics include the fact that the solution is organisationally dependent, and that the model allows for alternate production characteristics at the operating levels.

The organisational dependence of the GGD model implies that the resource allocation solution obtained is a satisficing one. This is a reflection of the fact that the solution is not global in the sense of a single objective, but rather a function of multiple and competing divisional goals and priorities. Given the genuine potential for gaming in the model, just as in all similar models, resultant resource allocations can be sub-optimal. For example, divisions can manipulate their resource allocations by assigning different priorities to the goals of specific resources. By according a higher priority to the goal of resource X, a division can obtain higher amounts of that resource than is warranted by its technology requirements. *Ex-post* reviews of the goal resource mix can lead to reduced levels of gaming, but as in most models of this kind it is impossible to avert gaming altogether.

The model, however, offers the potential for participation in the decision-making process by lower organisational units, since it is based on sub-unit goal priorities and resources, rather than being solely dependent upon data transmission. Against this it can be argued that lower-level participation may be more apparent than real, since central management can influence the responses of divisions through the manipulation of the shadow prices. Further, the model integrates resource allocations with operating activities for all sub-units in the organisation, thereby avoiding the artificial separation of resource allocation from other organisational activities as is usually the case in models focusing exclusively on resource allocations.

SUMMARY

The main objective of this chapter has been to examine the literature on capital resource allocation and investment decisions in divisionalised organisations. The analysis has drawn extensively on the markets and hierarchies literature, emphasising in particular the various mechanisms of monitoring capital investment decisions advocated by Williamson. Further, historical evidence and the results of a number of cross-sectional empirical studies of capital resource allocation practices were analysed to shed further light on the problems of resource allocation and use. Finally, a formal general model of resource allocation, the generalised goal decomposition model (GGD) was discussed.

Several important results have emerged from the analysis presented in this chapter. First, although the capital market and the market of corporate control exert powerful, and in general highly effective, influence on most firms, divisionalised organisations are less susceptible to, and appear to have less need for, such control mechanisms. Indeed, given the properties of divisionalised organisations, their organised internal markets, and the wide-ranging and complex array of accounting and administrative control mechanisms they employ, there are strong sreasons to argue that the M-form arrangements should supplant both capital markets and the market for corporate control in a variety of settings.

Second, the in-depth historical investigations and the aggregate cross-sectional results of resource allocation practices reveal a wealth of information which give some indication of why the M-form structure has been so dominant. The evidence points strongly towards the emergence of powerful accounting and administrative mechanisms which both monitor and coordinate the flow of capital resources in divisionalised organisations in an efficient and parsimonious, if not always serendipitous, manner. These non-market mechanisms have evolved to mitigate the considerable costs of exclusive reliance on pure market principles, and thus to internalise transaction gains within hierarchies. The preceding section contains a description of a model (the GGD model) which illustrates how these control mechanisms can operate to monitor and coordinate capital resource allocation within divisionalised organisations. These findings also offer useful insights into the extent to which corporate practices reflect acute awareness of many of the serious limitations of highly abstract prescriptions, by developing allocation schemes rooted in the organisational context. Such contrasts and tensions between theory and practice could be mobilised to shed further light on worthy future research developments in this field.

A major limitation of the analysis undertaken in this chapter is its focus on rationalistic scenarios of resource allocation and use. As is already widely recognised, decision-making in organisations is frequently driven by arguments other than those espoused by the proponents of rational behaviour. Capital resource allocation and use can be guided by political, symbolic, and ritualistic considerations, and these clearly deserve further scrutiny (see Feldman and March, 1981). Moreover, the analysis has focused on financial measures, to the exclusion of other quantitative, non-financial measures and qualitative indicators. This latter deficiency is explored further in the following chapter.

APPENDIX 4.1

The GGD model for a divisionalised organisation with the above hierarchic structure would involve M divisional managers (DM) reporting to central management (CM), and N operating unit managements (OM) reporting to divisional manager k, and will be of the following form (see Bailey and Boe, 1976 for this adaptation):

1. (CM) Maximise

$$\sum_{f=1}^{F} \sum_{k=1}^{M} \Pi_{kf} G_{kf}$$

subject to

$$\sum_{k=1}^{M} P_{kf} G_{kf} \leq G_{of}; \quad f=1,\ldots,F$$

$$G_{kf} \geq 0; \quad k-1,\ldots,M; \quad f=1,\ldots,F$$

2. (DM$_k$) Minimise

$$\sum_{f=1}^{F} (W^+{}_{kf} Y^+{}_{kf} + W^-{}_{kf} Y^-{}_{kf})$$
$$+ \sum_{r=1}^{K} (V^+{}_{kr} E^+{}_{kr} + V^-{}_{kr} E^-{}_{kr})$$

subject to

$$\sum_{j=1}^{N_k} A_{jkf} X_{jk} - Y^+{}_{kf} + Y^-{}_{kf} = G_{kf}; \quad f=1,\ldots,F$$

$$a7.5 \sum_{j=1}^{N_k} B_{jkr} X_{jk} - E^+{}_{kr} + E^-{}_{kr} = C_{kr}; \quad r=1,\ldots,R_k$$

$$X_{jk}, Y^+{}_{kf}, Y^-{}_{kf}, E^+{}_{kr}, E^-{}_{kr} \geq 0$$

$$j=1,\ldots,N_k; \quad f=1,\ldots,F; \quad r=1,\ldots,R_k$$

3. (OM$_{jk}$) Minimise

$$\sum_{f=1}^{F} \Pi_{kf} A_{jkf} + \sum_{r=1}^{R_k} \Pi'_{kr} B_{jkr}$$

subject to

$$\sum_{f=1}^{F} D_{jkfq} A_{jkf} + \sum_{r=1}^{R_k} D'_{jkfq} B_{jkf} \geq S_{jkq}; \quad q=1,\ldots,Q_{jk}$$

$$A_{jkf}, B_{jkr} \geq 0; \quad f=1,\ldots,F;, \quad r=1,\ldots,R_k$$

Where:

Π_{kf}	represents the shadow prices of dual values relative to corporate goals f
G_{kf}	represents the role of division k in meeting goals f
G_{of}	represents the goals of the whole organisation
P_{kf}	represents the specification of the contribution to the attainment of goals f
Y^{+}_{kf}, Y^{-}_{kf}	represent positive and negative deviations from goals specified by central management
W^{+}_{kf}, W^{-}_{kf}	represent the weights reflecting priorities for positive and negative deviations from goals f
E^{+}_{kr}, E^{-}_{kr}	represent positive and negative deviations of goals pursued by division k but not specified by central management
V^{+}_{kr}, V^{-}_{kr}	represent the weights reflecting priorities for positive and negative deviations from goals r
A_{jkf}	represents the quantity of goal f used by operating unit$j$ofdivision$k$w4.5
X_{jk}	represents the quantity of product j that division k should produce
B_{jkr}	represents the quantity of goal r used by operating unit j of division k
C_{kr}	represents the values for division k of pursuing goals other than those specified by central management (r)
Π_{kr}	represents the shadow prices relative to the division's chosen goals r

D_{jkfq}, D'_{jkfq}, S_{jkq} represent the coefficients expressing the relationships between divisional resources which could be mutually substitutable.

The responsibilities of each of these three hierarchical levels, as depicted in Figure 4.1, are as follows. Corporate management (CM) determines the goals of the organisation which can include profits, resource usage, prices, etc. and whose values are denoted G_{of} for $f = 1, \ldots, F$. Linear programming models are used by corporate management to determine the role of each division in meeting those goals. The role of division k in meeting goal f is denoted by G_{kf}, and the specification of its contribution to the attainment of that goal is denoted by P_{kf}. Corporate management determines divisional goals by maximising the values of the goals to the divisions using the prices Π_{kf}, which were discussed in more detail earlier.

Each divisional manager determines how resources provided can be used to attain the goals set by corporate management. Each division has a multiple goal problem reflecting the activities of its N_k operating units. Each operating unit j specifies the quantity of its product or the activity level for its project which requires a given amount of resource f or yields a profit to meet goal f. The quantity of goal f used by operating unit j of division k is denoted by A_{jkf}.

Divisions may pursue goals other than those specified by corporate management, R_k, whose values for division k are C_{kr}, and for whom the quantity of goal r used by operating unit j of division k is denoted by B_{jkr}. The divisional manager uses the model to determine the quantity that should be produced of product j, X_{jk}, with the aim of minimising the deviations from goals, Y^+_{kf}, Y^-_{kf}, E^+_{kr} and E^-_{kr}. Priorities are determined for each goal, and weights reflecting them are assigned to the deviations, W^+_{kf}, W^-_{kf}, V^+_{kr} and V^-_{kr}.

The operating unit management (OM) may represent a product, a group of products or a project. OM determines the materials and other resources needed for its planned activities. Q_{jk} represents the constraint set faced by the j operating management, and the coefficients D_{jkfq}, D'_{jkfq} and S_{jkq} express the relationships between resources and the extent to which their mutual substitutions are possible. The operating management aims to determine the level of its activity and the optimal resource mix which minimises the cost, or shadow prices $\Pi_{k\,f}$ and $\Pi_{k\,r}$ given to it by the divisional manager.

QUESTIONS

1. Describe and critically evaluate the theoretical arguments pertaining to resource allocation in divisionalised organisations.
2. Provide an overview of the historical evidence relating to the allocation and monitoring of resources in divisionalised companies. Comment on the extent to which you think such evidence helps inform theory.
3. Summarise and evaluate available questionnaire-based evidence on resource allocation and monitoring in divisionalised companies. To what extent is this evidence consistent with theory?
4. Explain and evaluate the basic attributes of the generalised goal decomposition (GGD) model developed by Ruefli. To what extent do you think this model can significantly improve resource allocation in practice?
5. Available evidence indicates that optimal, but complex models, such as decomposition models, are not widely used in practice, and yet most divisionalised companies seem to be successful. Explain how, if at all, these two observations can be reconciled.

5

Beyond Financial Measures of Divisional Performance

The analysis in the previous chapters has focused exclusively upon the design and use of a wide-ranging set of financial controls, the ultimate aim of which is to bring the diverse interests of divisional managers in line with those of top management. As indicated earlier, many of these controls are highly sophisticated, and they are particularly effective when used as part of a package of control, as evidenced from the practices of the pioneering firm General Motors. However, this exclusive focus on financial measures has two major limitations. Firstly, it ignores the important role that other quantitative, non-financial controls can play in guiding the performance of local managers. Secondly, by implication it completely understates the extent to which qualitative controls bring about organisational coherence and reduce the potential for opportunistic behaviour.

This chapter seeks to address these two deficiencies by discussing explicitly the roles of quantitative, non-financial controls and qualitative controls in the context of divisionalised organisations. As will soon become apparent, there is a serious paucity of research in these important areas. Hence, the level of analysis will of necessity be less rigorous than in the previous chapters.

In the following section, a more explicit statement will be made concerning the inadequate consideration of non-financial and qualitative controls in the markets and hierarchies framework. This is followed by an examination of control through structural arrangements, for example through restricting divisional size or curtailing the decision-making autonomy of divisional managers, and manipulating reward structures by the use of non-financial criteria such as seniority. There follows a discussion of non-financial, but quantifiable measures of performance such as market share, customer service, output targets, and product quality control. The penultimate section is devoted to an examination of qualitative controls such as those based on leadership style, culture, traditions, and common values and beliefs. The final section contains a summary of the chapter.

NON-FINANCIAL CONTROLS IN THE MARKETS AND HIERARCHIES FRAMEWORK

To explore the role of non-financial controls in the literature on markets and hierarchies, reference is made first to the main tenets of this framework. According to its proponents (Williamson, 1970; 1975; 1981; Ouchi, 1979; 1980), the notion of transactions cost is central to the analysis. Indeed, it has been argued that the main contribution of that framework draws from its ability to operationalise transactions cost in a manner which facilitates measurement of the efficiency of alternative modes of mediating transactions (Spicer and Ballew, 1983). According to that framework, hierarchies supplant markets when it is more economical to organise transactions within hierarchies. The emphasis is therefore on quantifying the costs of transactions in financial terms, for this would be deemed necessary before the transactions costs of alternative governance structures could be compared. Hence, the development of a financial metric of transactions is assumed to be a fundamental notion in the literature on divisionalisation.

However, this presumed emphasis on financial metrics and calculative relations has been questioned even by Williamson

(1975), the chief architect of the markets and hierarchies theory. He has suggested that, in contrast to markets, internal organisation (i.e. the divisional form) is more suited to making allowance for "quasimoral involvement among the parties" (p. 38). Because differing exchange relations arise from differing corporate governance structures (e.g. markets, hierarchies) and because these relations are valued, Williamson (1975, p. 39) appeals for the concept of organisational effectiveness to be conceived more broadly than is implied in the conventional efficiency calculus:

> Thus, modes of organization or practices which would have superior productivity consequences if implemented within, and thus would be adopted by a group of expected pecuniary gain maximisers, may be modified or rejected by groups with different values . . . .. In addition, preferences for atmosphere may induce individuals to forego material gains of non-pecuniary satisfactions if the modes of practices are regarded as oppressive or otherwise repugnant.

For Williamson then, internal organisation provides an exchange atmosphere which is less calculative than that provided by markets. These arguments are reflected to some extent in the set of normative and informational requirements for control under internal organisation. "Normative requirements" refer to the basic social agreements shared by the exchange parties in order to minimise transactions cost. "Informational requirements" are those postulated to match the normative requirements of the particular mode of control. Ouchi (1980) identifies two normative requirements for control in hierarchies: reciprocity in exchange relations, and legitimate authority. Reciprocity promotes equity and fairness in exchange; legitimate authority facilitates the use of hierarchical control, not only to assign tasks to employees but also to regulate and monitor their performance. Ouchi argues that reciprocity is a universal norm, and that legitimate authority is accepted by employees in formal organisations, albeit in varying degrees. The informational requirements are reflected in organisational rules. In comparison with prices, the informational requirement in the case of markets, rules tend to be problem-specific and they tend to be formalised for routine decisions. When exceptional situations are encountered they are typically referred to policy makers at the top of the hierarchy, who frequently have to invent new rules as the situation demands.

While the above discussion may indicate a relatively less calculative tradition in internal organisation compared with markets, it should be noted that such tradition is still highly calculative, in the main explicitly formal, and hierarchical. In this setting, prevailing accounting controls tend to be rooted in a hierarchic, top-down philosophy of control. They would involve the use of highly calculative systems which emphasise financial measures of performance for monitoring behaviour (budgets, standard cost systems, financial measures of performance such as profit, ROI, and residual income, internal audit procedures, administrative internal pricing systems, frequent performance reports, and financial reward schemes). Such systems are not only highly calculative, but they are also explicitly hierarchical and formal. To be sure, there are some discussions of less formal and less hierarchical controls in the internal organisation literature, but these are the exception rather than the rule.

For example, Williamson (1970, p. 129) has briefly referred to the pressures which can be exercised by lower-level participants on deviant divisional managers to bring their behaviour into line with corporate policy in order to avert cuts in divisional resources that may be imposed as a penalty by headquarters. The rationale offered by Williamson for this behaviour is that lower-level participants are usually amongst the first to suffer the consequences of cuts in divisional resources, which could result in job losses or at least temporary loss in income. Further, Williamson has alluded to the usefulness of non-financial reward systems which are suited to divisionalised organisations, such as promotion on the basis of seniority. However, it has to be emphasised again that these are exceptional examples and that the extant literature on divisionalisation promotes controls which are predominantly calculative, financial, and short-term. The only other obvious exception to the financial emphasis relates to a broader body of literature which has sought to identify some of the *structural* controls that can be deployed by headquarters to increase their control over divisional managers; these are discussed briefly below.

STRUCTURAL CONTROLS IN DIVISIONALISED ORGANISATIONS

Following the lead of the markets and hierarchies literature, the accounting literature on divisional control has been concerned almost exclusively with the development of financial measures of performance. In the few cases where structural controls have been addressed, the analysis has been neither comprehensive nor rigorous. This is one of the most serious drawbacks in the divisional accounting literature. In contrast, divisional control as defined here emphasises financial and structural control devices, both formal and informal, quantitative and qualitative. These different control devices interact with and, to a certain extent, constrain each other.

In the context of divisionalised organisations the overall control apparatus can encompass a variety of measures. These may relate to: (a) defining divisional environment; (b) determining divisional size; (c) defining and coordinating divisional interdependencies; (d) determining the extent of divisional decision–making autonomy; (e) defining the characteristics of information and of information flow; (f) designing an internal audit system; and (g) designing an appropriate reward system. Such characteristics may be viewed by organisational participants as a set of interacting decision variables which constrain their action, as well as being the subject of their own manipulations. Each of these means of control has an important role to play in harmonising the activities of various company divisions and in achieving some form of overall organisational coherence.

In order to achieve the required or "permissible" degree of control over some of these variables, the central management would typically make use of some set of administrative rules, as well as various informal measures. Formal administrative rules have been the focus of some considerable attention in the management science, economics and organisation theory literatures. Bonini (1964), for example, has advocated the notions of "control-in-the-large" and "control-in-the-small". The former comprises rules and procedures which concentrate on the totality of the firm and lead to greater measures of decentralisation, whereas the latter deals with segments of the firm and prescribes detailed standards of performance. Similarly, Arrow (1964) has advocated the notions of "operating rules" and "enforcement rules" to deal with the specification of decision criteria and the monitoring and evaluation of performance.

In the organisation theory literature, divisional control is seen by some (Lorsch and Allen, 1973) as being attainable through the judicious use of differentiation and integration. According to Lawrence and Lorsch (1967), differentiation refers to differences in goal, time and interpersonal orientations and in formality of practices amongst managers in different organisational units. Integration refers to the quality of collaboration existing amongst organisational units required to achieve unity of effort. In contrast, informal control measures have rarely been considered explicitly, particularly in the accounting and economics literatures. In this section the control implications of the structural characteristics outlined above are discussed, emphasising some of the formal and informal control measures suggested in the literature.

Divisional environment

Lawrence and Lorsch (1967) have reported that: (a) the degree of differentiation required in the firm depends on the extent of diversity of its environment: the more diverse the environment, the more differentiated the sub-units (e.g. divisions, business units) are likely to be; (b) the difficulty of attaining integration is a function of the extent of differentiation: the more differentiated any two sub-units are, the more difficult it is to achieve integration between them.

The above argument implies that the more the divisions operate in diverse environments, the more difficult it is to integrate their activities because of the greater requisite differentiation between them. It is plausible to assume that it would be desirable, at least from the point of view of the central management, for the divisional control system to facilitate the attainment of the requisite degrees of differentiation and integration.

Lorsch and Allen (1973) have considered the influence of the environment on organisational practices, human relations, and performance evaluation systems; see Table 5.1. They reported that

TABLE 5.1 A summary of Lorsch and Allen's results

Environmental dimension/ *characteristics*	*Impact on practices*
A. Corporate-divisional level	
+ Diversity:	+ Differentiation
+ Diversity:	− Integration
+ Interdependence	+ Complex integrative devices
+ Interdependence and	
− diversity:	+ Integration effort
− Interdependence:	− Size of headquarters
	− Complex integration
	+ Speed of response to divisional requests
B. Organisational characteristics	
+ Fit between environment and differentiation/integration:	+ Balance of cognitive orientations of divisional integrators
	+ Influence of divisional integrators
	+ Quality of information
	+ Confrontation to resolve divisional conflict
C. Divisional level	
+ Uncertainty:	+ Formalisation
+ Diversity, complexity and competitiveness:	+ Differentiation
+ Interdependence:	+ Complexity of integration devices
D. Performance measurement	
Conglomerates:	+ Explicitly defined criteria
	+ Linkage between performance and monetary rewards
	+ Emphasis on financial, end/result criteria
Vertically integrated:	+ Informality of performance evaluation
	− Link between performance and monetary rewards
	+ Emphasis on financial, end/result criteria *and* operating intermediate criteria

+: increase in
−: decrease in

within each division, functional (operating) units tended to develop organisational practices which were consistent with the state of the environment. Thus: (a) greater uncertainty in divisional environments resulted in more formalised organisational practices, and (b) greater diversity, complexity, and competitiveness of divisional sub-environments resulted in higher differentiation within the division. Similarly, the extent of differentiation amongst divisions seems to be influenced by the diversity of divisional environments in a manner analogous to that of functional units. The degree of central-divisional differentiation has been reported by Lorsch and Allen to be positively related to the extent of diversity of the firm's total environment. Furthermore, cognitive limits of managers at both headquarters and divisional levels, and greater environmental diversity, seem to restrict the degree of central-divisional integration.

It is worth noting that differentiation can only reduce, but not eliminate, the consequences of divisional interdependence. To manage interdependence more successfully, the organisation needs to achieve some degree of integration between its divisions. Here again, the findings of Lorsch and Allen (1973) provide some useful insights in the context of divisionalised organisations. Their results point to three major sets of factors which are reported to be related to the effective management of differentiation and integration, namely integrative devices, integrative effort, and decision-making processes. They reported that both within divisions and at corporate-divisional levels, more complex patterns of interdependence among the relevant divisions resulted in the emergence of more complex integrative devices.[1] Their findings also suggest that at corporate-divisional level greater interdependence associated with lower diversity calls for greater integrative effort in order to manage inter-divisional relationships appropriately.

Lorsch and Allen have also indicated (in consistency with Lawrence and Lorsch, 1967) that some of the characteristics

---

[1] According to Lorsch and Allen, integrating devices may be classified in terms of increasing complexity into paper systems (e.g. budgets), integrative positions (e.g. divisional specialists at headquarters), committees, task forces, and formal meetings and direct managerial contact.

of effective decision-making are independent of the particular environmental requirements, whilst others are contingent upon prevailing environmental forces. In organisations characterised by patterns of differentiation and integration which are consistent with their environmental settings, persons performing inter-divisional and corporate-divisional integration were reported to have cognitive and interpersonal orientations that were balanced amongst those divisions they were expected to integrate. They also tended to have greater influence compared with members of these divisions, irrespective of environmental contingencies. Further, the researchers reported that such organisations were characterised by a flow of high-quality information, and that they resorted to confrontation as a means of resolving inter-divisional conflict.

Decision-making characteristics that were contingent upon the environment included speed of headquarters' response to divisional requests, distribution of influence over decision-making, and divisional performance evaluation systems. The results indicated that the lower the interdependencies required by the environment, the smaller the corporate headquarters units, the less complex the integration devices and information transmission, and the more rapid the headquarters' response to divisional requests tend to be.

Lorsch and Allen further considered some of the characteristics of divisional performance measurement systems. They reported that conglomerates employed performance evaluation systems that were characterised by explicitly defined criteria, a direct linkage between performance and monetary rewards and greater emphasis on financial/end result criteria. Vertically integrated firms, faced with lower diversity and uncertainty but higher interdependence, developed performance evaluation systems that were more infor-mally administered without a direct linkage between performance and monetary rewards and with emphasis on both financial/end result and operating intermediate criteria.

Divisional size

Implications for the optimal sub-unit (divisional) size, from the perspectives of economic efficiency of production, information transmission, and control, have been examined in the economics and management science literatures (see, for example, Lioukas and Xerokostas, 1982). In general, this literature suggests that economic units with similar technological and structural characteristics have comparable optimal economic size.

Yet, this may not always be the case in reality. Economic efficiency may not be the only consideration guiding the decisions of the central management in determining divisional size. Cultural, political, and societal considerations may have significant influences. Moreover, even if the central management aims at attaining optimal economic size in pursuit of economic efficiency, divisional managers may have a vested interest in managing larger divisions in order to maximise their non-pecuniary benefits, or in order to increase the extent of formal and informal control they exert upon the parent organisation. Conversely, the central management (and other divisional managers) may oppose expansion in the size of a particular division, in order to restrict the power that can be wielded by its manager. Divisional size is then an important control variable which may be the subject of frequent manipulations both by the central management and by divisional managers. The resulting size may be as much a reflection of compromise and historical incidence as the outcome of economic and administrative efficiency arguments.

Divisional interdependence

In the context of divisionalised organisations, it is expedient to consider levels and types of interdependence. Levels of interdependence refer to positions in the organisation's hierarchy at which interdependence may occur. A convenient way of depicting this is to collapse the hierarchy of a divisionalised organisation into a small number of essential organisational levels. Although there are several alternatives, Ruefli (1971a) provides a useful scheme, discussed in more detail in the preceding chapter, in which he distinguishes between three levels: (a) central management; (b) divisional management and (c) operating units within each division. Therefore, there are at least four sets of relationships which would reflect interdependencies:

1. The relationships between central management and each divisional manager.
2. The relationships between managers of different divisions.
3. The relationships between every pair of operating units within a division.
4. The relationships between divisional management and each of its operating units.

Other relationships could be considered, e.g. between the operating units of different divisions, but these are assumed away, for simplicity. At each of the three specific levels several forms of interdependence may occur:

1. Demand interdependence: complementary; competitive (see, for example, Hirshleifer, 1957).
2. Technological interdependence: pooled; sequential; reciprocal (see, for example, Thompson, 1967).
3. Behavioural interdependence: unidirectional; bidirectional; multidirectional (see, for example, Ruefli, 1971b).

Without "appropriate" coordination of such interdependencies, inefficient, and even adverse, decisions may be taken. For example, when the demand for the products of company divisions is competitive, some divisional managers may engage in opportunistic practices (e.g. significant price reductions) which further their own interests at the expense of those of other divisions and of the company as a whole. Similarly, when the technologies of some divisions are sequentially or reciprocally interdependent the flow of activities between these divisions has to be carefully coordinated.

Lorsch and Allen (1973) have provided some useful insights relating to managing interdependence. They considered divisional differentiation at three levels: within each division; between divisions; and between each division and the central management. Their results indicate that interdependence is higher among functional (operating) units within a division, than amongst divisions or between divisions and the headquarters. Their observation has important implications for the design of divisionalised organisations. Thus, in the face of complex and uncertain environments, the organisation may be able to confine complex interdependencies within divisional units, while permitting less complex interdependencies to exist either between the divisions and the headquarters or amongst the divisions. This leaves managers at each level with the relatively easier task of managing a limited portion of the firm's total environment. It is worth noting, however, that containing complex interdependencies within divisions has implications for other divisional control variables. For example, this may lead to changes in divisional size, the definition of divisional tasks, the identification of lines of authority and responsibility, and so on.

In their historical analysis of administrative practices, Chandler and Daems (1979) found that as task interdependence increased, there was less reliance on market mechanisms to coordinate activities. Instead, administrative coordination mechanisms within the plants were developed to cope with problems of interdependence. Accounting systems were designed to facilitate such coordination, including "sophisticated cost accounts and detailed operating statistics in the case of transportation, stockturn in distribution, and the ticket-system in production" (Chandler and Daems, 1979, p. 9). These were accompanied by the development of new accounting concepts such as operating ratio, unit costs, and standard costs.

Divisional autonomy

Divisional autonomy underlies a number of important control issues. For instance, it can play a crucial role in the evaluation of alternative performance measures (see, for example, the Solomons/Amey debate regarding whether or not a cost of capital figure should be levied against divisional revenues, which was discussed in some detail in Chapter 2). Moreover, it may be closely associated with overall company effectiveness and other organisational characteristics. There are a number of key questions that may be asked in this connection. For example, how much autonomy should divisional managers have in a given decision-making area? What considerations should be taken into account in deciding upon that degree of autonomy? Should the degree of autonomy in the same decision area differ for different managers? And so on.

Unfortunately, the literature in this area is sparse. Some of the relevant conceptual problems have been alluded to. Examples include problems of quantifying discretion and assigning appropriate weights to different decision areas (e.g. Leibenstein, 1965; but see Ezzamel and Hilton, 1980b). Moreover, Williamson (1970; 1975) has considered the question of how decision-making responsibility should be divided between the headquarters and divisional managers. He has stipulated that responsibility for decision-making should be split between divisional managers and central managers, so that the former handle operating decisions whereas the latter focus on strategic decisions. Any confounding of such a distinction he contends, will result in sub-optimal divisionalisation which will, in turn, have detrimental effects on company performance. This argument is supported by the historical analysis of the practices of pioneering divisionalised organisations such as General Motors and Du Pont (Chandler and Daems, 1979, pp. 14–15).

At General Motors and Du Pont, as became true of new enterprises adopting the new multi-divisional form, the top line executives were relieved of all day-to-day operating responsibility. These tasks were left to the division managers and their line departmental executives. Assisted by a large financial and advisory staff (organized along functional lines), the general executives concentrated on monitoring divisional performance in terms of rate of return on investment (using Donaldson Brown's formula) and market share. They spent even more time allocating resources on the basis of these evaluations and on increasingly sophisticated forecasts and detailed capital budgets provided by both operating divisions and specialists on the advisory staff. Freed from operating duties and no longer representing functional departments, the general executives had a more positive psychological commitment to the future of the enterprise as a whole.

Thus, if central managers become directly involved in operating decisions, a corrupted divisionalised structure emerges in which at least four types of decision-making inefficiency may occur. Firstly, inferior operating decisions are likely to be made because central managers are not as well informed as are divisional managers, in operating matters. Secondly, operating decisions may be untimely if, as would be expected, central managers have to wait for local information to be collected and submitted to them. Thirdly, communication channels will be overloaded by information transfers from divisional managers to central managers and vice versa, leading to greater system noise and cost. Fourthly, strategic decisions will be of poorer quality because central managers, being immersed in operating matters, would be unable to devote the requisite time and attention to such decisions. Similarly, if divisional managers become directly involved in strategic decisions, overall company survival could be endangered because these managers lack the corporate view required for making such decisions, and may also pursue interests that are detrimental to corporate interests.

A decision-making area of prime importance is that relating to the allocation of resources amongst divisions. This, Williamson has argued, is the prerogative of central management, who can effectively replace and even outperform the external capital market by regulating the divisionalised firm as a miniature capital market; see the detailed arguments in Chapter 4. Rather than allowing newly generated cash flows to simply revert back to the divisions where they have been realised, they are exposed to internal competition and are ultimately allocated to those divisions with the potentially most profitable investment proposals. Thus, resource allocation is made responsive to differential performance.

The implications of such a resource allocation system for divisional control are significant. Resource commitments are clearly essential for divisional continuity and growth. Financially successful divisions are likely to command greater resources which, in turn, could lead to greater size and importance. Moreover, divisions with tendencies to conform less with central policies could be brought into greater conformity with such policies through the resource allocation system. Less conformity could imply less resources being allocated to the division. This may lead to pressure being exerted on divisional managers by lower-level participants, to avoid penalties that could be imposed by headquarters, as suggested earlier.

How do these theoretical arguments compare with empirical results? In general, available empirical evidence is neither comprehensive nor conclusive. Several studies (e.g. NICB, 1961; Mauriel and Anthony, 1966; Tomkins, 1973; Ezzamel and Hilton, 1980a; 1980b; Scapens and Sale, 1981; 1985) have attempted to provide some assessment of the extent of divisional autonomy in several decision-making areas, but few have attempted to relate their findings to other organisational characteristics, e.g. technology or environment. This body of evidence suggests that the extent of divisional autonomy varies greatly from one decision-making area to another. Thus, it appears that divisional managers enjoy greater discretion with respect to operating policy decisions, and less discretion in the areas of financing policy, investment policy and accounting and internal control systems (see Ezzamel and Hilton, 1980b; Tomkins, 1973). The results of Scapens and Sale (1981), however, suggest that divisional managers may be able to influence capital investment decisions, even though such decisions are typically subject to formal authorisation by higher managers (for counter-arguments, refer to the discussion in Chapter 4).

Although this descriptive evidence is useful, it clearly fails to provide answers to questions such as: why should the extent of discretion vary between decision-making areas? Is there an optimal level of divisional discretion, and if so, how can it be defined? A common-sense approach would presumably imply that divisional discretion should be limited in decision areas characterised by excessive interdependencies, as well as in areas of central importance to the organisation as a whole. This may be particularly crucial if, as is frequently the case, the performance evaluation system employed by the organisation does not reflect fully the consequences of decisions taken by divisional managers. Is there much evidence in support of such common-sense argument?

Here again, available evidence is limited and inconclusive. A useful contribution in this context is the work of Lorsch and Allen (1973). They reported that in organisations characterised by appropriate patterns of differentiation and integration, the distribution of decision-making power, both lateral and hierarchical, tended to coincide with the location of relevant information. Thus, at the corporate–divisional interface, influence tended to be concentrated at divisional management level in conglomerates which were faced with higher uncertainty and diversity and lower interdependence. In contrast, in vertically integrated organisations, senior vice-presidents exercised greater influence on decision making, and this naturally resulted in a contraction in the degree of autonomy enjoyed by divisional managers.

In a study undertaken by Ezzamel and Hilton (1980a) the authors attempted to investigate: (a) the association between divisional discretion (autonomy) and other company characteristics, and (b) the question of optimal divisional discretion. Their results suggest that there is little difference in the extent of overall divisional discretion across different industrial classifications.[2] They noted, however, that companies in their sample with outside markets for all their products seemed to operate with greater measures of divisional autonomy, compared with companies which had outside markets for only some of their products. This may be rationalised on the grounds that in the absence of an outside yardstick, greater central control may be required to motivate divisions to act in accordance with overall corporate interest. Scapens and Sale (1985), however, tested for the possibility that differences in divisional autonomy contribute to the variety in accounting methods used to control divisionalised operations. Such expected association was not observed in their results. The results of Ezzamel and Hilton also suggest that their own sample of UK companies seemed to have operated with sub-optimally high degrees of divisional discretion: the estimated probability of company success for their sample rose as the autonomy score fell.

Characteristics of information and information flow

One of the important implications of agency theory and of the markets and hierarchies theory for the design of accounting systems is their focus on the characteristics and flow of information. Information has been advanced by these theories as an effective means for the reduction of uncertainty. *Ex-ante* information reduces *ex-ante* uncertainty (arising from the agent taking actions before their consequences reveal themselves) by helping the

---

[2] It should be noted, however, that the industrial classification was rather broad, and hence different insights might have emerged had finer industrial classifications been used.

divisional manager to predict future states of the world. *Ex-post* information reduces *ex-post* uncertainty (arising from inability to identify determinants of outcome) by facilitating the writing and enforcement of contracts between headquarters and divisional managers: "the knowledge that such information will be available, *ex-post*, enables *ex-ante* agreements to be reached by the contracting parties" (Tiessen and Waterhouse, 1983, p. 258).

Specific information characteristics could facilitate the reduction of uncertainty. *Ex-ante* information should be predictable, and thus it should be possible to obtain and harness it in order to reduce uncertainty. *Ex-post* information should be verifiable, unequivocal and acceptable to relevant users. These characteristics minimise disputes in performance evaluations which may arise in the context of a division in relation to measurement of outcomes, causes of outcomes and other dimensions of performance (Tiessen and Waterhouse, 1983).

The nature of information may also vary, depending on prevailing conditions. Thus, in situations where it is possible to write and enforce complete employment contracts between headquarters and divisional managers, the focus of the accounting system would be on providing the detailed information necessary for complete contracting. However, in other situations (i.e. where the writing and enforcement of complete contracts is not possible), information about output becomes more important. When output is difficult to observe and verify, owing to high levels of technological and environmental uncertainty, the focus of information is likely to shift towards "soft" information about divisional technology and environment, corporate ethos, managerial seniority, and so on (Spicer and Ballew, 1983).

Internal audit and reward systems

As suggested in Chapter 4, internal audit can involve performance evaluation at three levels: advance, contemporaneous and *ex post*. Advance evaluation involves reviewing divisional proposed alternative courses of action and forming judgements as to their merits, cost and overall desirability. Contemporaneous evaluation entails continuous monitoring of current divisional performance against some previously stated target. *Ex-post* evaluation involves comparing divisional actual performance against targets at the end of a given period.

Williamson (1970; 1975) has argued that internal audit systems in divisionalised organisations are more effective than the external capital market in controlling divisional activities for two reasons. Firstly, the relationships between divisional managers and central managers are regulated through employment contracts. As a consequence, the records and files of divisional managers, as subordinates, are directly available for review by central management. Much of this information is not disclosed to outsiders and thus capital markets cannot engage in comparable evaluations. Secondly, internal disclosure of information is usually assumed to be an essential feature of organisational cohesiveness and integrity, and it is thus expected to foster greater cooperation between organisational participants. In contrast, disclosure of internal information to outsiders (unless authorised) is not viewed favourably by the organisation.

The reward system is another means through which the management of the divisionalised company can regulate and motivate divisional activities towards desired ends. Rewards may be pecuniary or non-pecuniary; both types can be adjusted by the headquarters to reflect differences in performance and to bring divisional activities in line with corporate policy. The reward system can be structured in such a way that persistently deviant (uncooperative) divisional managers are penalised through job transfers, or even dismissal. Moreover, as Williamson (1975) has noted, managerial changes at divisional level are frequently undertaken because they lead to better motivation of lower-level participants; hence they tend to be engineered in a way which is conducive to bringing about 'desirable' behavioural consequences. Employment policies, including employment contracts, can be specified and organised in a way that maximises the chances of divisional activities being kept in line with corporate interest.

The preceding discussion illustrates the wide-ranging repertoire of controls which are available to divisionalised organisations. It is clear from the discussion that financial control, which has long been cherished in the accounting literature as the most important form of control, is only a subset of that repertoire. Moreover, the controls discussed above are not mutually exclusive: rather, they complement each other. Further, instead of endorsing the contingency view of deterministic matchings between situational contingencies and control devices (see Ezzamel and Hart, 1987, Chapter 4), the above discussion emphasises the considerable choice of controls available to divisionalised organisations.

NON-FINANCIAL, QUANTIFIABLE PERFORMANCE MEASURES

The discussion in the previous section focused on the design and use of structural controls which seek to define the feasible region within which divisional managers can exercise their decision-making power. In a sense, these structural arrangements reflect an attempt by the headquarters of the divisionalised company to control the activities of its divisional managers through *exclusion*, for by defining what they can do, the headquarters is also by implication indicating what decisions they should *not* make, and which business arenas they should not enter. By contrast, the discussion in this section focuses on quantifiable non-financial measures which seek to motivate the behaviour of divisional managers towards specific and more precise organisational ends.

The call for the use of non-financial, quantifiable performance measures is not new; it has underlined much of the literature which has sought to expose the limitations of short-term financial measures of performance in divisionalised organisations (see, for example, Ezzamel and Hart, 1987). The problem is, however, that these calls have been, and remain, expressed in vague exhortations which offer little comfort to those seeking to apply them.

One example is that provided by Parker (1979). After elaborating some of the limitations of conventional divisional performance indices and indicating the drawbacks of relying only on any one index, Parker (1979, p. 317) calls for supplementing conventional measures through the use of a wide-ranging set of non-conventional measures:

Further attention could usefully be paid to the development of divisional productivity indices, projected monetary benefits of the maintenance of certain market positions, costs versus benefits of product development, division social accounts for social responsibility, and human resource accounting for aspects such as personnel development, employee turnover, accident frequency, etc.

A more recent example is the influential book by Johnson and Kaplan, *Relevance Lost* (1987). After constructing an apparently powerful argument in which they criticise contemporary management accounting systems for being irrelevant to the needs of the modern enterprise, they propose their own "recipe" to regain lost relevance. As part of this "recipe", they devote the last chapter in their book to a discussion of "performance measurement systems for the future", in which they seek to further expose the limitations of short-term financial measures, and then to make a case for the importance of non-financial indicators. But the problem is not how to make a case for non-financial measures, since the case has been established for some time; rather, the problem is how to devise and elaborate credible measures. Their very brief discussion of the whole issue (just over three pages) is therefore much less helpful than one initially suspects. Their main arguments in this context are discussed below.

Johnson and Kaplan argue that non-financial indicators should be driven by corporate strategy, and should include key measures of manufacturing, marketing, and research and development success. In a sense, they are advocating a contingency theory notion which involves establishing a fit between non-financial indicators and the precise strategic posture of the organisation. For example, if the strategy is to be a lower-cost producer the company should develop productivity measures which show trends in their ability to produce more while utilising the same, or fewer production factors. And although the company may be able to achieve higher profits in the short run through increased price recovery (because of output prices rising at a faster rate than input prices), the focus must be on seeking to achieve long-term productivity gains. In contrast, if quality is the focus of corporate strategy, the company should evolve and use non-financial indicators which reflect internal failure – such as scrap, rework, defects, machine breakdowns – as well as external failure indicators, reflecting customer complaints, warranty expenses, and service calls. In contrast, companies which emphasise innovative and high-performance products should develop non-financial indicators which reflect total launch time for new products, key characteristics of new products such as speed or durability, and customer satisfaction with products. Through the judicious matching of non-financial indicators with corporate strategy, Johnson and Kaplan assert that companies would become more competitive, particularly if in the mean time they could rid themselves of short-term financial measures.

In a sense, as Johnson and Kaplan (1987, p. 259) themselves state, a move towards non-financial measures and away from short-term financial measures would signal a return to cost management practices of the nineteenth century, which relied on operation-based measures. But such a move will also be consistent with the current practices of many Japanese companies. The need for such non-financial measures has become more critical following the advent of the new, wide-ranging, innovations in work technology and information technology. As Bromwich and Bhimani (1989, pp. 56–7) have pointed out:

> Within the new manufacturing environment, monitors of quality, delivery time, inventory reduction and machine performance are seen as replacing measures of labour productivity, machine and capacity utilisation and standard cost variances. Accordingly, information systems need to shift their focus from traditional quantitative financial data to operating quality and other measures.

This call has been repeated frequently, and some attention has been devoted to developing coherent operations-based measures. An example of this is the set proposed by Howell and Soucy (1987) which emphasises quality, inventory, material scrap, equipment maintenance, and delivery throughput. A list of some of the non-financial measures which are relevant to each of these five categories is contained in Table 5.2, in addition to a further four categories which seem plausible (clearly this is *not* an exhaustive list): flexibility, human relations, safety, and industrial relations.

It has also been suggested that conventional methods of investment appraisal are not appropriate for companies utilising

TABLE 5.2 Examples of operations-based performance measures

Category	Non-financial measures
I. *Quantity*:	1. Records of customer complaints. 2. Customer satisfaction. 3. Levels of warranty claims. 4. Monitoring the quality of services and components from vendors, suppliers and subcontractors. 5. Statistics on scrap, rework and returns.
II. *Inventory*:	1. Records of the number of inventoried items. 2. Warehouse space utilisation and planned reductions. 3. Material turnover rates by product and location.
III. *Material scrap*:	1. Incoming material inspection records. 2. Measures of scrap by part, product, and operation. 3. Scrap as a percentage of total output.
IV. *Equipment maintenance*:	1. Machine usage statistics. 2. Equipment performance. 3. Capacity utilisation. 4. Machine breakdown and maintenance.
V. *Delivery throughput*:	1. Delivery times. 2. Order fill rates. 3. Lead and process times. 4. Set-up times. 5. Production backlogs. 6. Average set-up times. 7. Average number of days' production in inventory. 8. Average distance travelled by products in the factory. 9. Percentage of delivery commitments met in each period.

TABLE 5.2 Continued

Category	Non-financial measures
VI. *Flexibility*:	1. Total number of parts per product. 2. Percentage of common parts versus unique parts in products. 3. The number of sub-assembly or bill of materials levels.
VII. *Human relations*:	1. Absenteeism. 2. Staff turnover. 3. Recruiting success. 4. Morale. 5. Skills. 6. Career progression.
VIII.*Safety*:	1. Number of consecutive days without accidents. 2. Number of workdays lost due to accidents.
IX. *Industrial relations*:	1. Number of workdays lost due to strikes. 2. Percentage of conclusive wage settlements without arbitration. 3. Proposition of employee representations on major boards and committees.

advanced manufacturing technology, because some of the important benefits are not readily quantifiable. These could include improved quality, higher machine reliability, faster delivery, lower after-sale maintenance requirements, greater production flexibility, and faster throughput (Bromwich and Bhimani, 1989). Moreover, some of the benefits are likely to extend into the long run, but with higher uncertainty in relation to benefit level, precise timing, and effect in relation to various functions such as ordering and processing. This deficiency is exposed further in those situations where capital investments in new technology have a radical impact on production arrangements, resulting for example in significant changes in the layout and design of plants. These difficulties have led Bromwich and Bhimani (1989, pp. 58–9) to argue:

> Such strategic investment decisions need to be handled differently from more tactical short-term decisions so as to encompass not only cash flow forecasts but also the longer-term strategic aspects of intended projects within the overall perspective of the firm.

The importance of this strong appeal is acknowledged, but here again there are only a few guidelines as to how this can be achieved. Bhimani and Bromwich (1988; 1989) propose combining formal and informal analyses of capital investment within a strategic investment appraisal framework by linking corporate strategy to the perceived benefits from the investment, in the manner advocated by Johnson and Kaplan, as suggested earlier. Bhimani and Bromwich suggest (1989) that perceived benefits from investment are categorised into: (a) those which are readily quantifiable financially; (b) those which can be quantified financially but with some effort, and (c) those which cannot be quantified in financial terms. The three categories are then ranked in the context of a strategic planning matrix, giving three scores for each investment proposal. Examples of non-quantifiable investment benefits include (Bromwich and Bhimani, 1989, p. 60):

> quality improvements, increased production flexibility and customer satisfaction, enhanced company image and reduced risk through greater product mix possibilities and broader skills range . . . . Synergies across plants and divisions and new information exchange possibilities between different advanced manufacturing systems within the organisation.

As can be seen from the above discussion, the tendency of most contemporary accounting researchers is to adhere to the notion that, although there might be a potentially long list of non-financial indicators, individual firms have to be selective by linking explicitly their choice of indicators to their corporate strategy. Despite the attractiveness of this argument, those who either find the concept of strategy problematic or who do not accord strategy such an elevated position would encounter serious difficulties in benefiting from the argument. More critical, perhaps, is the underlying unidirectional causal links which are presumed to exist between the non-financial indicators and strategy, as implied by the contingency theory model. As contingency theory has been subjected to severe and wide-ranging criticisms (see Ezzamel and Hart, 1987, Chapter 4 for a review), these will clearly apply to the above arguments. Further, in the main the recommendations involve little more than a simple listing of possible indicators, without any serious attempt to explore more fully how they can actually be implemented and what implications this would have on organisational performance. Finally, qualitative measures are hardly discussed; a look at Table 5.2 shows that only a brief listing has been attempted, and even then those which have been identified are hardly discussed in the literature. It is this latter point which is the main focus of the next section.

QUALITATIVE CONTROLS

Some useful insights on the use of non-accounting information in the context of performance evaluation can be gleaned from the work of Hopwood (1972; 1974). He distinguished between three styles of using budgeting information in the evaluation of managerial performance: budget-constrained style, profit-conscious style, and non-accounting style. The first two styles make use of budgetary information, the major difference being that the budget-constrained style focuses on the manager's ability to continually meet short-term budget targets, whereas the profit-conscious style focuses on the ability of the manager to improve the operations of a sub-unit (e.g. a division) in a manner which is consistent with the long-term objectives of the parent company. By contrast, the non-accounting style makes little use of budgetary information in the context of managerial performance evaluation. Whilst Hopwood's research was not concerned with the details relating to the precise types of information used under the non-accounting style, it does offer fascinating insights relating to their behavioural implications. For example, in contrast to the budget-constrained style, the use of the non-accounting style was associated with: (a) lower job-related tension and lower manipulations of accounting reports; (b) better relations with superiors and colleagues (in the case of superiors, this was reflected in greater trust in and respect for supervisors, greater satisfaction with supervisors' administrative, technical and human relations skills, and greater appreciation of the reasonableness of supervisors' expectations. In the case of peers, this was manifest in better peer-supportiveness, achievement and affiliation; better peer agreement, helpfulness and friendship; and better respect for peers); and (c) better job satisfaction and feelings of justness of evaluation.

The above discussion could be interpreted as embracing issues related not only to leadership style but also to corporate culture. One of the major differences between control through internal organisation and control through clans (or corporate culture) is that under the former traditions, based on common values and beliefs, are not admitted in the analysis as a significant informational requirement for control. Instead, emphasis is placed upon rules, and as indicated earlier, rules tend to be formalised and problem-specific, allowing little scope for the qualitative dimension of performance (Ouchi, 1980). If increased elements of corporate culture are permitted into the internal organisation model, so that a hybrid emerges, the relevant set of normative requirements can be extended to include common values and beliefs, in addition to reciprocity and legitimate authority. This would accord traditions greater importance as an informational requirement of control.

Common values and beliefs are established and sustained over long periods of time and are usually subscribed to by those who have been members of the organisation for a reasonably long period. New members would tend to go through a gradual process of organisational socialisation so that their consensus over these values and beliefs is also attained gradually. Almost invariably, common values and beliefs are informal and mostly unwritten, their power emerging from their being ingrained into the memories of organisational participants and also from being widely reflected in organisational practices. Traditions, as an informational requirement of control, are much cruder and less sophisticated than either prices or rules. Once common values and beliefs are constituted into a coherent culture, they gain greater visibility, both within and outside the organisation. Corporate culture, while being the subject of social and political influence within the organisation, can become a potent control tool in the hands of management, in terms of monitoring and disciplining lower-level managers. To the extent that some elements of culture can be manipulated, top management can motivate the performance of lower managers (e.g. divisional managers) in the directions that they desire. This, however, will be curtailed by the extent to which lower-level managers can resist such potential manipulations. What is critical, however, is that irrespective of how it is constituted, corporate culture can be used to propel the organisation towards the successful realisation of its basic mission. Potential divergences between corporate goals and those of its participants can frequently be minimised, as they become internalised into the widely accepted culture; hence selfish and opportunistic behaviour can be significantly curtailed.

Elements of the organisation's culture and of its dominant values and beliefs can be reflected, in part, in the leadership styles adopted by managers. In this context, organisational socialisation is also likely to take place at higher managerial levels. As organisational values and beliefs are "accepted", albeit somewhat revised, by other managers, their diffusion into the organisation is then facilitated through managerial practices and prevailing leadership styles. For example, an organisation whose cultural focus is a "friendly and supportive work environment" would tend to encourage managers to adopt an "initiating" leadership posture in which emphasis is placed on informal relations and employee-oriented matters (Ezzamel and Hart, 1987).

SUMMARY

The main purpose of this chapter was to explore some of the non-financial measures and monitors of performance that are relevant in the context of divisionalised organisations. The analysis commenced with an examination of the role of non-financial controls in the literature on markets and hierarchies. It was suggested there that although the literature assumes that internal organisation (i.e. divisionalised structures) promotes an exchange atmosphere which is inherently less calculative than that provided by markets, such a research tradition still espouses controls which are highly calculative, formal, and hierarchical.

This was followed by a discussion of the roles played by various structural controls in monitoring divisional performance. These included such constraining factors as environmental dimensions of the division, divisional size, divisional interdependence, divisional decision-making autonomy, characteristics of information and information flow, and internal audit and reward systems. It was suggested there that, within certain limits, the headquarters can judiciously manipulate these variables in a manner that could bring about some 'desired' changes in the practices of divisional managers. Quite how successful the headquarters would be at achieving such ends depends upon, among other things, the extent to which they can manipulate some exogenous factors, such as external environmental forces, and the extent of power that is wielded and can be exercised by divisional managers. The important observation which emerges from the analysis in that section is the availability of a wide-ranging repertoire of controls which are suited to divisionalised organisations, of which financial control is only a sub-set.

The following section dealt with non-financial, but quantifiable measures of performance. It was suggested there that the need for such measures had been recognised long ago and that the major challenge lay rather in designing and applying them. An emerging argument in the field is for such non-financial but quantifiable measures to be explicitly derived from corporate strategy and for them to reflect performance in the organisation's key areas: manufacturing, marketing, and research and development. Although a long list of such measures can now be drawn, it is clear that the list is fairly *ad hoc*, and also that the list may not be that helpful to practitioners, since the burden of choosing from the available alternative measures is left to the individual company. It is not therefore clear whether some of these measures are, in principle, more optimal than others, and what dysfunctional consequences could be associated with their use.

The penultimate section provided a necessarily brief discussion of qualitative performance-monitoring systems – in particular traditions, common values and beliefs, corporate culture, and managerial leadership style. These parameters develop over relatively long periods of time and, once established, tend to be fairly robust. They can, however, be manipulated in various ways in order to enhance the extent of control exercised by the headquarters over divisional managers and, in turn, by these latter managers over their subordinates.

To the extent that many of these non-financial quantitative and qualitative controls are used by companies, as appears to be the regular practice of Japanese companies and more increasingly of Western companies, this offers an interesting contrast to the academic literature. For far from arguing, as has frequently been the case in the recent past, that corporate practices are lagging behind academic developments, it appears that practitioners have established an incisive lead over academics in a number of critical applications. Academics can no longer afford to ignore these developments in their research deliberations.

A number of important conclusions emerge from the analysis in this and the preceding chapters. First, control in the context of divisionalised organisations, in common with other organisations, should be conceived fairly broadly as denoting organisational, rather than simply management, control. In this case, organisational participants are preoccupied not only with the conventional notions of hierarchical control but also, and equally importantly, with issues of organisational coherence and structural design. Second, and this emerges from the first conclusion, it should be recognised that there exists a wide-ranging repertoire of controls which are of immediate relevance to divisionalised organisations; these are not only financial, but are also structural, non-financial quantitative, and qualitative. Third, these controls are not mutually exclusive, but can, and should, be used in combinations. Fourth, more attention should be focused on developing more non-financial measures, both of the quantitative and qualitative varieties, employing methodologies which are less *ad hoc* than those currently in use. The relevance of much of the above, however, depends to a large extent upon the future viability of the divisionalised form of organisation. This is discussed briefly in the next chapter.

QUESTIONS

1. To what extent are non-financial measures, both quantitative and qualitative, discussed in the mainstream literature on markets and hierarchies?

2. Identify and explain some of the structural controls which are relevant to organisations designed along the multidivision or business unit lines. Evaluate the effectiveness of these structural controls in contributing to overall corporate success.
3. Contrast the sets of non-financial, quantitative measures most suited to: (a) a lower-cost producer, and (b) an innovation leader. What limitations, if any, do these measures have?
4. It has been suggested that the non-financial measures most suited to any firm are those which are directly derived from that firm's strategy. Comment.
5. Explain the role of qualitative controls in monitoring the performance of divisionalised companies.

6

Summary, Implications and Future Developments

The main concern of this book has been to provide a synthesis of the literature on performance measurement in the context of divisionalised organisations, that is for such sub-units as business units and divisions. The divisionalised form of organisation which emerged in the early part of this century has been the most prevalent organisational form, at the very least in the context of North American and Western European economies. The wide use of this structural form has given rise to numerous accounting issues that differ significantly from those facing other structural arrangements, such as the centralised form. These issues include transfer prices, reward schemes, and performance measurement and evaluation; the latter being the focus of our attention here. A significant number of eminent researchers and practitioners have devoted much of their attention to the development of alternative measures of divisional performance, the ultimate aim of which is to reconcile two conflicting objectives: (a) aligning the interests of sub-unit (e.g. divisional) managers with those of central management, and (b) permitting sub-unit managers significant levels of autonomy with respect to operating decisions. The emerging performance measures have several ingenious properties.

Yet, they also have numerous dysfunctional consequences for corporate long-term performance. These attributes, both favourable and dysfunctional, have been discussed in some detail in the preceding chapters and are summarised below.

This brief concluding chapter seeks to draw together the main arguments contained in the previous chapters, to examine some of the implications of these arguments, and to consider some of the future implications relating to the impact of recent developments in information technology and global competition on the future of the divisionalised form of organisation. The chapter is therefore divided into three main sections, dealing consecutively with these three issues.

SUMMARY OF PREVIOUS CHAPTERS

The main purpose of this book has been to provide a synthesis of the diverse literature on performance measurement of business units and divisions, and to focus attention on some of the dilemmas encountered therein. Many of the issues which have been raised in the previous chapters relate quite directly to some of the issues raised in other volumes in this series. In particular, the present volume should be considered as complementary to *Transfer Pricing: Theory and Application*, and *Performance Evaluation and Incentive Schemes*, and strongly related to *Capital Investment Appraisal*.

Given the well-specified objectives of this volume, emphasis has been focused on providing a critical technical appraisal of the so-called traditional accounting measures of performance, contrasted against theoretically optimal models, both in the context of operating decisions and capital budgeting decisions. As part of the technical appraisal undertaken here, explicit reference is made to the limitations of financial measures of performance and to the important role that can be played by non-financial measures, both quantitative and qualitative. This book draws on contributions from industrial economics, accounting, business history, and management science. It should be noted, however, that reference to these diverse literatures had necessarily to be brief, as space limitations do not permit full elaboration of the arguments. This volume should therefore be viewed as a concise statement on performance measurement in divisionalised organisations; readers interested in the details are advised to consult the original references cited in this book and elsewhere.

Having provided some indication of the main purposes and the context of this book, it is instructive to follow this by offering a summary of the main arguments contained in the preceding chapters.

Chapter 1 was mainly concerned with clarifying some of the essential terminology and considering the case for and against the multidivision form. Distinctions were drawn between some related concepts, with the difference between centralisation and decentralisation revolving mainly around the extent to which decision-making power is devolved to lower managerial levels, and the difference between these two and divisionalisation focusing on whether or not sub-unit managers have responsibility for specific profitability targets. Distinctions were also drawn between various forms of responsibility centre, such as business units, cost centres, profit centres, investment centres, and revenue centres. The main emphasis in the discussion there was on the cost/revenue flow and the extent to which this can be traced to an individual, a collectivity of individuals, or a sub-unit.

The case for the multidivisional form rested on its major attributes in the face of problems caused by large size, and more importantly by product and market diversity. These attributes centre around the design and use of: (a) an internal miniature capital (and labour) market which displaces the external capital (and labour) market in the mediation of many transactions; (b) a performance evaluation system (internal audit) which emphasises advance, contemporaneous, and *ex-post* aspects of managerial performance; (c) a finely tuned reward scheme which aligns divisional interests with those of the whole corporation. These attributes, in addition to the careful separation and allocation of strategic and operating decisions to different managerial levels, lead to least cost and profit-maximising behaviour. These achievements seem to be supported by the prevalence, and apparent persistence, of the multidivisional form in North American and Western European economies. Against this it has to be remembered that the multidivisional form can trigger off costs of its own, caused for example by intensive competition between sub-units and by the need to attain and integrate the activities of differing but interdependent sub-units. Further, as is argued below, there are alternative, and at least equally plausible, means of dealing with diversity.

Chapter 2 dealt with traditional accounting-based measures of performance: accounting profit, return on investment (ROI), residual income, and sales forecasts. These indices are extremely popular among practitioners, but it has been shown that each of them has some serious limitations which are index-specific, and also that all of them share some serious common limitations. Very briefly, the most pertinent and critical index-specific limitations are:

1. Accounting profit does not account explicitly for the cost of using capital resources, and thereby its use will quite likely result in some divisions making greater use of corporate resources which can be used more profitably elsewhere (either as internal or external investments).

2. ROI focuses managerial attention upon maximising percentages. This has the likely impact of demotivating managers from undertaking *all* profitable alternatives (from a corporate point of view), since this will inevitably be inversely related to divisional ROI. Division managers will therefore be motivated to operate their divisions at levels below those deemed optimal from a corporate point of view.

3. While residual income appears to make up for some of the major deficiencies of both accounting profit (by explicitly levying a cost of capital charge) and ROI (by promoting a profit level rather than a percentage), it falls short of being a suitable index of performance. In particular, the derivation of the cost of capital, as advocated by Solomons (1965) and others, is fraught with both conceptual and practical problems.

The problems which are commonly shared between all these indices are as follows:

Short-termism All indices are focused on short-term performance measurement, to the exclusion of the long term. This has the undesirable effect of encouraging opportunistic behaviour by managers whose consequences are only revealed in the long term.

Past orientation All these indices reflect *past* managerial actions; while this may be of some relevance for control purposes, they are inappropriate for decision-making, which should be future-oriented.

Measurement problems All indices rely on conventional accounting procedures regarding overhead allocation, valuation, recognition, periodicity, and so on; these may not be suitable for the measurement of sub-unit performance.

Chapter 3 examined "ideal", but abstract, measures of performance. Initially, the discussion centred around an examination of the attributes of the "ideal" concept of income rooted in the notion of maximisation of shareholders' wealth. The concept of discounted cash flow (DCF) was then examined in the context of its approximation to "ideal" income and of the major problems which have to be encountered in utilising a DCF-based construct of performance measurement. These problems related to the underlying assumptions of the model, model formulation, measures of divisional (business unit) risk, and the calculation of divisional cost of capital. Reference was made to the possible use of the capital asset pricing model (CAPM), but applied to non-traded securities, to derive estimates of divisional cost of capital which reflect the differing risk profiles of independent divisions.

The main conclusions which emerged from the discussion in Chapter 3 were as follows:

1. DCF-based income offers a sound proxy for "ideal" income and, at least in theory, can be adapted to reflect the performance of sub-units and their managers.
2. Despite its conceptual superiority, DCF-based income is hardly, if ever, used by divisionalised companies for the purposes of performance measurement.
3. Most likely, the main reason for the lack of popularity of DCF-based income measures among practitioners, despite its widespread appeal among academics, is the inherently difficult,

perhaps even insurmountable, challenges posed by its attempted application. In particular, the most daunting problems relate to generating reliable estimates of future cash flows and of divisional cost of capital. It was suggested in Chapter 3 that this reasoning may explain, but should not necessarily justify, the lack of DCF popularity among practitioners. All indices of performance, conventional (as discussed in Chapter 2) and non-conventional alike, have serious reliability problems. DCF-based measures, while having their fair share of reliability problems, are at the very least conceptually more appealing.

Chapter 4 was concerned with monitoring capital budgeting decisions in divisionalised companies. The analysis commenced by reference to the theoretical guidelines of capital investment decisions in the markets and hierarchies literature. It was stated there that the most fundamental attribute of the multidivisional form is the establishment and use of an internal miniature capital market. This mechanism ensures that capital is allocated to high-yield uses by requesting divisions to bid against each other, offering detailed calculations of projected profitability rates for each project. Rather than allowing cash flows to revert back to the divisions from which they originated, as under the centralised form, the headquarters scrutinises and ranks divisional bids and then allocates funds on the basis of such ranking.

Evidence from detailed business history studies and from empirical, questionnaire-based surveys, indicates that fund allocations and authorisations of capital use are typically restricted where most of the power resides in the hands of central management. Moreover, in the few cases where divisional managers enjoy some discretion over such funds, and certainly in relation to the process of committing funds to capital projects, most companies operate fairly elaborate formal monitoring schemes seeking to minimise the scope for opportunistic behaviour by divisional managers. These include the careful scrutiny of divisional investment proposals by capital appropriation committees, and the operation of advance, contemporaneous, and *ex-post* audits of various kinds. These controls seek to (a) ensure that funds are *optimally* invested − that is, deployed in the most profitable investment projects; and (b) ensure that once committed, capital investments are optimally managed and utilised.

It was indicated there, however, that such emphasis on calculative, rational modes of investment decision-making and appraisal fails to take account of the behavioural, political, and symbolic motives which could yield investment decisions insusceptible to sensible explanations if rational choice models alone were invoked. A more complete understanding of the complex process of capital investment decisions requires the impact of these forces to be brought to bear on any analysis undertaken.

Chapter 5 dealt with non-financial measures of divisional performance; this involved both quantitative and qualitative measures. It was noted there that, with few exceptions, the markets and hierarchies literature is characterised by a conspicuous absence of any significant examination of non-financial, and more particularly qualitative, measures of performance. Except in those cases where mention is made of possible informal pressure being exerted by subordinates over their own divisional managers to act in consistency with corporate interests, thereby avoiding possible sanctions that could impact more heavily upon them, and of the use of direct observation and seniority in promotion decisions, the emphasis is predominantly on financial, quantifiable measures of performance.

The chapter explored a set of structural controls, the aim of which is to curtail divisional power by reducing the opportunity set within which it can legitimately operate; as such this is a form of *preventive* control. These controls include determining divisional size, defining the domain and level of divisional autonomy, drawing the boundaries between different divisions and identifying divisional/environmental interface, designing internal audit systems, and modelling reward schemes which promote consistency between divisional interests and those of the corporation.

Other quantifiable, non-financial measures of performance were discussed. These seem to emanate from the emergence of new work and information technologies which have resulted in radical changes in work practices with significant implications for operating and investment decisions. Examples relating to the operating decisions category include statistics on factory safety, employee turnover, and customer satisfaction; those relating to capital investment decisions include linking such decisions to corporate strategy and using non-conventional investment appraisal procedures. These techniques have apparently been used for some time by Japanese companies and are being used increasingly by Western companies.

Chapter 5 then considered the role of qualitative measures of performance, focusing more explicitly on issues such as corporate culture and leadership style. It was stated there that although these concepts are not susceptible to sensible, short-term quantification, they nevertheless play a critical role in engineering consensus, and in engendering subordinates' loyalty. They should therefore be treated as an important element of a widely conceived notion of control.

In the penultimate section of this chapter, we provide an explorative, and highly tentative, discussion relating to the future of the multidivisional form, and consider some of the implications of these possible developments for the design of accounting systems in divisionalised organisations. But before we do this we examine briefly the implications of the previous analysis.

IMPLICATIONS OF PREVIOUS ANALYSIS

Having provided a synthesis of much of the literature on performance measurement in divisionalised organisations, a central question which should be addressed is what implications does this literature have for (a) the management of divisionalised organisations, and (b) research in this particular field?

The importance of this double question emanates from the observation made earlier in this volume, and summarised briefly in the preceding section, to the effect that performance measurement systems used by many divisionalised companies are technically highly deficient, are poor proxies for "ideal" performance measures, and are incomplete in scope (because of the lack of well-developed non-financial quantitative and qualitative measures). Against this, one has to note both the prevalence and apparent persistence of the multidivisional form. To the extent that well-designed accounting systems are a prerequisite for the success of organisational form, the above observation implies a contradiction, for how can one justify the success of the multidivisional form when its observed formal accounting systems are so highly defective? An alternative explanation could be quite simply that accounting systems are not critical to the success of structural forms.

This latter possibility, which may appeal to some commentators, is unlikely to be credible, for at least three reasons. First, it is much too easy an argument to invoke, for it seems more straightforward to dismiss the relevance of something when the linkages are not clearly visible, than to seek to establish difficult explanations for the unobserved linkages. Second, the suggestion that accounting does not matter to the success of the multidivisional form runs against the grain of the markets and hierarchies literature. In that literature, it will be recalled, accounting systems are assumed to play a central role in the development and operation of internal miniature markets for labour, capital, and goods, and in the effective use of internal audit systems and reward structures. Third, much of the literature on the contingency theory of management accounting points to the strong linkage and the quality of fit between structural forms and characteristics of the accounting system.

But if the argument of the irrelevance of accounting systems to the performance attributes of structural forms is rejected, how can one reconcile the use of apparently defective accounting systems with the observed significant success of divisionalised companies? There is no easy, straightforward answer to this problematic question; rather it is more instructive to seek to answer the question gradually and incrementally. Below, we offer two sets of arguments which may help in formulating a more satisfactory answer.

First, it could be argued that if better accounting systems were employed by divisionalised companies, then their level of success could have been far greater than that so far observed. Empirical studies assessing the performance of divisionalised companies are *comparative*; thus success is measured in terms of comparing a company's record *before* and *after* divisionalisation, or of comparing the records of a sample of divisionalised companies against the records of a sample of companies using other structural forms. More ambitious measures of performance, that is a company's observed record against the record it *ought* to have achieved (if this can be sensibly quantified) may reveal more clearly the need for introducing significant improvements in accounting systems used in divisionalised organisations. This argument has particular credibility for two reasons: (a) the companies against which divisionalised companies are compared may employ either inferior, or at best non-superior accounting systems, and (b) the recent observed decline in the performance of the corporate sector in the UK compared with that in Japan and Germany may indicate that significant improvements in accounting systems could enhance corporate performance.

Second, given the evidence cited in the previous chapters, it can be reasonably argued that divisionalised companies are well aware of the deficiencies of conventional performance systems and their awareness is reflected in their use of *multiple* performance indices *in addition* to other hierarchical, structural and qualitative controls. Certainly, while much of the academic effort in this field in the 1970s was bedevilled by the quest for the best *single* performance index which would attend to all users' needs, as far back as the 1920s pioneering companies such as General Motors combined the use of ROI with monthly sales forecasts, along with executive bonus schemes and tight procedural controls.

THE FUTURE: SOME FURTHER IMPLICATIONS

The discussion provided thus far has been based on the taken-for-granted assumption of both the prevalence and the persistence of the multidivisional form of organisation. Whilst the evidence on the prevalence of divisionalisation over the last few decades has been overwhelming, there are now emerging arguments which suggest that this structural form may be beginning to lose favour, and could be supplanted by other, more suitable structural forms. But before we discuss the extent to which the current persistence of the multidivisional form is under serious threat, it would be instructive to reflect, albeit briefly, on the conditions which gave rise to this particular organisational form, and to also refer to the extent to which these conditions can be "negotiated" through the use of alternative structures.

It will be recalled that the divisionalised form emerged in order to help management cope with the problems arising from large size and, more importantly, geographic and product diversity (Chandler, 1962; Williamson, 1970; 1975). Large size creates problems relating to sheer volume; these, however, could be handled satisfactorily by centralised structures through the judicious use of standard operating rules and procedures and through the deployment of increased levels of administrative and support staff. Large size *alone*, therefore, is *not* a prerequisite for the emergence of divisionalised structures.

The problems posed by diversity, however, are much more challenging than those posed by large size. Diversity introduces significant measures of uncertainty into the decision-making process. As technical expertise becomes more localised (for example, owing to significant increase in the number of different product lines), central management finds it increasingly more difficult to make informed and timely operating decisions. One approach to deal with this problem is that developed by Alexander Hamilton Church, during the scientific management era at the beginning of this century (see Vangermeersch, 1986). His approach was to use strategic product costing, rather than divisionalised structures, as a means of managing diversity. He advocated the use of product cost information to trace corporate-level profits to the profits of individual products. Instead of endorsing conventional and arbitrary methods of allocating overheads to products, Church argued that information relating to the cost of a particular product should reflect the real resources used in making the product. To overcome some of the problems caused by product diversity, he suggested that the factory be divided into a number of "production centres", to which overhead costs are initially traced and subsequently allocated to individual products. Although he ultimately treated factory costs *and* selling costs as parts of product costs in order to be able to trace corporate-wide profits to the profits of individual products, Church urged that the two types of cost should be considered separately. This, he argued, was because factory and selling costs are driven by widely-differing conditions, and not because the first "attach" to products and the latter to time periods, as is conventionally assumed. By emphasising the differing conditions that drive each type of cost, as Johnson and Kaplan (1987, p. 55) paraphrasing Church, have pointed out, "accountants and managers focus attention on 'the *real* incidence [of expense] on particular jobs' – the differences in rates at which products consume resources".

Another alternative for dealing with diversity, and as it happened the *one* alternative that was to gain prominence above all others, is to develop divisionalised structures in which central managers focus mainly on strategic issues, whereas local managers have the power to deal with operating decisions. As indicated in the preceding chapters, the latter is achieved through the utilisation of a carefully designed control package (a miniature internal capital market which effects the assignment of cash flows to high yield uses, an internal audit system, and a reward system), and with the help of advisory staff and divisional controllers who are attached to head office and who ensure that the interests of divisional managers are aligned with those of central management (Williamson, 1970; 1975).

We have already examined the extent to which these controls are successful in attending to the problems of managing diversity, and also in minimising the scope and potential for divisional managers to behave opportunistically. As indicated repeatedly before, these controls go a long way towards achieving these objectives, but there remains a real potential for dysfunctional consequences, mostly of the unintended kind. Many of these consequences can be averted if a broader concept of control is adopted in which attention is focused not only on formal, financial controls but also on other quantifiable, non-financial measures and, more importantly, on qualitative measures of performance.

But what of the future of divisionalisation? What is to become of the most prevalent organisational form of our time (at least among large and medium sized companies)? Accumulated evidence to date, though still highly incomplete, seems to indicate a move away from large, divisionalised firms, towards the "unbundling" and "downsizing" of these organisations. More specifically, the argument indicating a move *away* from divisionalisation is underpinned by two main reasons:

1. Recent economies in the cost of information processing,
2. Recent improvements in market efficiency.

Economies in the cost of information processing and transmission have recently become possible as a result of two parallel developments. The first relates to the invention of more efficient and more economical computers. The second relates to developments in data management which make possible the arrangement of data into hierarchies, allowing instant and constant access, as well as information-sharing among a multitude of users. These two developments combined have resulted in significant economies in information processing, and hence one of the main arguments in support of the emergence of divisionalised structures (information economies) appears to have been seriously undermined.

The second, and equally important, reason relates to the reported significant improvements in the extent of efficiency of capital markets, for both managers and capital. Capital markets now appear to exhibit greater levels of efficiency, and this has two main implications: first, an increased incentive for managers to act less opportunistically, as a result of the powerful sanctions that can be imposed by managerial labour markets; this reduces the need for the design and implementation of intricate internal mechanisms for effecting managerial sanctions and rewards through hierarchical arrangements. Second, a significant improvement in the ability of the capital market to allocate capital among competing firms (i.e. collectivities of investment proposals) seriously weakens, or even renders redundant, the need for an internal miniature capital market.

These arguments then suggest that the conditions which gave rise to the emergence of the large divisionalised firm have changed quite dramatically. The high costs of information processing and the highly inefficient managerial labour and capital markets that were characteristic of the 1920s have now been supplanted by more economical means of information processing and by more efficient markets for capital and labour. This seems to be consistent with the trends that emerged in the 1970s and which are still in evidence today: management buyouts, divestitures, and other "unbundling" and "downsizing" activities which have undermined significantly the model of the larger, multidivision firm. Further, the significant economies in information processing have led recently to a revival of interest in strategic product costing where, following Church, attention is increasingly being focused on tracing corporate-wide profitability to the profitability of individual products (Johnson and Kaplan, 1987).

Although the above arguments concerning the future of divisionalisation are highly speculative, and will have to remain so in the foreseeable future owing to lack of sufficient evidence, they do raise a number of intriguing implications for the design of accounting systems. Presumably, if the "unbundling" and "downsizing" of divisionalised organisations continues for an appreciable period of time, then centralised structures, or indeed other, perhaps even newly developed structural forms, will gradually replace divisionalised structures, and this could be accompanied by increased measures of market control, both over managers and capital. There could be less need for accounting systems to deal with some of the intractable dilemmas of transfer pricing; and to buttress hierarchical arrangements through the development of internal miniature capital markets, internal reward mechanisms, and internal audit systems. Indeed, accounting controls in divisionalised companies as we know them today would lose much of their conventional and familiar territories, as market-based controls encroach increasingly upon what has for so long been the sole preserve of accounting measures (Ezzamel, 1992).

SUMMARY

The main purposes of this final chapter have been to provide a summary of the previous chapters, to examine their broad implications, and to explore the potential impact of possible future developments on the viability of divisionalised structures, and by implication on their accounting systems. As indicated earlier, we have reviewed and evaluated a vast literature, dealing in the main with quantifiable, financial measures of divisional performance such as accounting profit, return on investment, residual income, and discounted cash flows. With the exception of the latter measure, these various measures of performance are characterised by several deficiencies emanating from "short termism", past orientation and measurement imperfections. On the other hand, while discounted cash flow measures are theoretically superior to conventional measures, they pose serious problems of implementation. It has also been argued that available non-financial quantitative and qualitative measures of performance are fairly crude, but that they have a critical role to play in monitoring divisional performance.

The literature reviewed here clearly has important implications. We have argued that accounting systems *do* matter to the efficiency of divisionalised organisations. It is imperative that designers of accounting systems strive to improve these systems, by seeking means of minimising their limitations and of rendering them more relevant. Until such improvements materialise, practitioners appear to be pursuing the best alternative available; that is, to use multiple measures, rather than seeking the ever-elusive best single measure, and to complement those with other quantitative non-financial and qualitative measures.

Finally, we explored some of the arguments relating to the possible impact of recent developments in information technology and work technology, the increased tendency towards deregulation of major services, the increased extent of local and global competition, and recent improvements in market efficiency on the future viability of divisionalised structures. It was stated there that alternative means of dealing with diversity and uncertainty include strategic product costing, and that recently there have been increasing calls for using this approach in preference to the divisionalised form. If this trend continues it is likely that the divisionalised form, and with it accounting systems designed specifically for this type of structure, will be on the decline. Given the lack of sufficient evidence, however, these arguments remain largely speculative.

Bibliography

Amey, L.R. (1969a), *The Efficiency of Business Enterprise*, London: George Allen & Unwin.

Amey, L.R. (1969b), "Divisional Performance Measurement and Interest on Capital", *Journal of Business Finance*, 1, Spring, pp. 1–7.

Amey, L.R. (1975), "Tomkins on Residual Income", *Journal of Business Finance and Accounting*, 2, Spring, pp. 55–68.

Arrow, K.J. (1959), "Optimization, Decentralization, and Internal Pricing in Business Firms", in *Contributions to Scientific Research in Management*, Western Data Processing Centre, University of California, January, pp. 9–17.

Arrow, K.J. and Hurwicz (1960), "Decentralization and Computation of Resource Allocation", in R.W. Pfouts (ed.), *Essays in Economics and Econometrics*, Chapel Hill: The University of North Carolina Press, pp. 34–104.

Arrow, K.J. (1964), "Control in Large Organizations", *Management Science*, 10 (3), April, pp. 397–408.

Ball, R. and Brown, P. (1969), "Portfolio Theory and Accounting", *Journal of Accounting Research*, Autumn.

Bailey, A.D. Jr. and Boe, W.J. (1976), "Goal and Resource Transfers in the Multigoal Organization", *The Accounting Review*, July, pp. 559–73.

Baumes, C.G. (1961), *Division Financial Executives*, Studies in Business Policy No. 101, National Industrial Conference Board.

Beaver, W., Kettler, P. and Scholes, M. (1970), "The Association Between Market Determined and Accounting Determined Risk Measures", *The Accounting Review*, October.

Bhimani, A. and Bromwich, M. (1988), *Strategic Investment Appraisal*, London School of Economics and Political Science (LSE), Working Paper.

Bhimani, A. and Bromwich, M. (1989), "Advanced Manufacturing Technology and Strategic Perspectives in Management Accounting", *European Accounting News*, January, pp. 21–31.

Bodenhorn, D. (1964), "A Cash-Flow Concept of Profit", *Journal of Finance*, March, pp. 16–31.

Bonini, C.P. (1964), "Simulation of Organizational Behaviour", in C.P. Bonini, R.K. Jaedicke, and H.M. Wagner (eds), *Management Control – New Directions in Basic Research*, McGraw-Hill.

Bower, J.L. (1970), *Managing the Resource Allocation Process: A Study of Corporate Planning and Investment*, Harvard University.

Bradley, A. (1926), "Setting up a Forecasting Program", *Annual Convention Series No. 41*, American Management Association, New York, pp. 3–20.

Bromwich, M. (1973), "Measurement of Divisional Performance – A Comment and an Extension", *Accounting and Business Research*, Spring, pp. 123–32.

Bromwich, M. and Bhimani, A. (1989), *Management Accounting: Evolution Not Revolution*, Research Studies, CIMA.

Brown, D. (1924), "Pricing Policy Applied to Financial Control", *Management and Administration*, 7, April, pp. 417–22.

Brown, P. and Ball, R. (1967), "Some Preliminary Findings on the Association Between the Earnings of a Firm, Its Industry, and the Economy", *Empirical Research in Accounting, Selected Studies*, Supplement to *Journal of Accounting Research*.

Chambers, J.C., Mullick, S. and Smith, D. (1971), "How to Choose the Right Forecasting Technique?", *Harvard Business Review*, July–August, pp. 45–74.

Chandler, A.D. (1962), *Strategy and Structure: Chapters in the History of American Industrial Enterprise*, Cambridge, Mass.: MIT Press.

Chandler, A.D. (1977), *The Visible Hand: The Managerial Revolution in Managerial Business*, Belknap Press.

Chandler, A.D. and Daems, H. (1979), "Administrative Coordination and Monitoring: A Comparative Analysis of the Emergence of Accounting and Organization in the USA and Europe", *Accounting, Organizations and Society*, 4 (1/2), pp. 3–20.

Dantzig, G.B. and Wolfe, P. (1963) "Decomposition Principle for Linear Programs", *Operations Research*, January–February, pp. 101–11.

Dearden, J. (1960), "Problems in Decentralized Profit Responsibility", *Harvard Business Review*, May–June, pp. 79–86.

Dearden, J. (1961), "Problems in Decentralized Financial Control", *Harvard Business Review*, May–June, pp. 72–80.

Dearden, J. (1969), "The Case Against ROI Control", *Harvard Business Review*, May–June.

Emmanuel, C.R. and Otley, D.T. (1976), "The Usefulness of Residual Income", *Journal of Business Finance and Accounting*, 3 (4), Winter, pp. 43–51.

Emmanuel, C., Otley, D. and Merchant, K. (1990), *Accounting for Management Control*, London: Chapman and Hall.

Ezzamel, M. (1979), "Divisional Cost of Capital and the Measurement of Divisional Performance", *Journal of Business Finance and Accounting*, 6 (3), Autumn, pp. 307–19.

Ezzamel, M. (1985), "On the Assessment of the Performance Effects of Multidivisional Structures: A Synthesis", *Accounting and Business Research*, 61, Winter, pp. 23–4.

Ezzamel, M. (1992), "Corporate Governance and Financial Control", in M. Ezzamel and D. Healthfield (eds), *Perspectives on Financial Control: Essays in Memory of Kenneth Hilton*, London: Chapman and Hall.

Ezzamel, M. and Bourn, A.M. (1988), "Why Do Firms Allocate Costs?" in J. Arnold, D. Cooper and R.W. Scapens (eds), *Case Study Research in Management Accounting*, London: ICMA.

Ezzamel, M. and Hart, H. (1987), *Advanced Management Accounting: An Organisational Emphasis*, London: Cassell.

Ezzamel, M. and Hilton, K. (1980a), "Divisionalisation in British Industry: A Preliminary Study", *Accounting and Business Research*, Spring, pp. 197–211.

Ezzamel, M. and Hilton, K. (1980b), "Can Divisional Discretion be Measured?", *Journal of Business Finance and Accounting*, 7 (2), Summer, pp. 311–29.

Fama, E.F. (1968), "Risk Return and Equilibrium: Some Clarifying Comments", *The Journal of Finance*, March.

Fama, E.F. and Jensen, M.C. (1983a), "Separation of Ownership and Control", *Journal of Law and Economics*, June, pp. 301–25.

Fama, E.F. and Jensen, M.C. (1983b), "Agency Problems and Residual Claims", *Journal of Law and Economics*, June, pp. 327–49.

Feldman, M.S. and March, G.M. (1981), "Information in Organizations as Signal and Symbol", *Administrative Science Quarterly*, 26, pp. 171–86.

Flower, J.F. (1971), "Measurement of Divisional Performance', *Accounting and Business Research*, 1 (3), Summer, pp. 205–14.

Fuller, R.J. and Kerr, H.S. (1981), "Estimating the Divisional Cost of Capital: An Analysis of Pure-Play Technique", *Journal of Finance*, December, pp. 997–1009.

Gabor, A. and Pearce, I.F. (1952), "A New Approach to the Theory of the Firm", *Oxford Economic Papers*, October, pp. 252–65.

Gonedes, N.J. (1969), "A Test of the Equivalent-Risk Class Hypothesis", *Journal of Financial and Quantitative Analysis*, June.

Gordon, M.J. and Halpern, P.J. (1974), "Cost of Capital for a Division of a Firm", *Journal of Finance*, September, pp. 1153–63.

Henderson, B. and Dearden, J. (1966), "New Sytem for Divisional Control", *Harvard Business Review*, September–October, pp. 44–60.

Hirshleifer, J. (1957), "Economics of the Divisionalised Firm", *The Journal of Business*, April, pp. 96–108.

Hopwood, A.G. (1972), "An Empirical Study of the Role of Accounting Data in Performance Evaluation", *Empirical Research in Accounting: Selected Studies*, Supplement to *Journal of Accounting Research*, pp. 156–82.

Hopwood, A.G. (1974), *Accounting and Human Behaviour*, London: Haymarket Publishing.

Horngren, C.T. (1962), *Cost Accounting: A Managerial Emphasis*, Englewood Cliffs, NJ: Prentice-Hall.

Howell, R.A. and Soucy, G.R. (1987), "Cost Accounting in the New Manufacturing Environment", *Management Accounting*, August, pp. 42–9.

Jaedicke, R.K. (1967), A Critique, in *The Use of Accounting Data in Decision Making*, T.J. Burns (ed.), Columbus, Ohio: Ohio State University.

Johnson, H.T. (1978), "Management Accounting in An Early Multidivisional Organisation: General Motors in the 1920s", *Business History Review*, L.11 (4), Winter, pp. 490–517.

Johnson, H.T. and Kaplan, R.S. (1987), *Relevance Lost: The Rise and Fall of Management Accounting*, Boston: Harvard Business School Press.

Joyce, J.M. and Vogel, R.C. (1970), "The Uncertainty in Risk: Is Variance Unambiguous?", *The Journal of Finance*, March.

King, P. (1974), "Strategic Control of Capital Investment", *Journal of General Management*, No. 2, pp. 17–28.

Lawrence, P.R. and Lorsch, J.W. (1967), *Organization and Environment – Managing Differentiation and Integration*, Harvard: Division of Research, Graduate School of Business Administration, Harvard University.

Lawson, G.H. (1971a), "Measuring Divisional Performance", *Management Accounting*, May, pp. 147–52.

Lawson, G.H. (1971b), "Cash Flow Accounting", *The Accountant*, October 28th, November 4th.

Lee, T.A. (1962), "A Case for Cash Flow Reporting", *Journal of Business Finance*, 4 (2), Summer, pp. 27–36.

Leibenstein, H. (1965), *Economic Theory and Organizational Analysis*, Harper and Row and John Weatherhill.

Lintner, J. (1965), "Security Prices, Risk and Maximal Gains from Diversification", *Journal of Finance*, December.

Lioukas, S.K. and Xerokostas, D.A. (1982), "Size and Administrative Intensity in Organisational Divisions", *Management Science*, 28 (8), August, pp. 854–68.

Lorsch, J.W. and Allen, S.A. III (1973), *Managing Diversity and Interdependence*, Division of Research, Graduate School of Business Administration, Harvard University.

Ma, R. (1969), "Project Appraisal in a Divisionalized Company", *Abacus*, December, pp. 132–42.

Mauriel, J. and Anthony, R.N. (1966), "Misevaluation of Investment Center Performance", *Harvard Business Review*, March–April, pp. 98–105.

Merchant, K. (1989), *Rewarding Results: Motivating Profit Center Managers*, Boston: Harvard Business School Press.

Mintzberg, H. (1979), *The Structure of Organisations*, Englewood Cliffs, NJ: Prentice-Hall.

Morgan, J. and Luck, M. (1973), *Managing Capital Investment*, Mantec.

Mossin, J. (1969), "Security Pricing and Investment Criteria in Competitive Markets", *American Economic Review*, December.

Moyer, R.C. (1970), "Berle and Means Revisited: The Conglomerate Merger", *Business and Society*, Spring, pp. 20–9.

NICB (1961), "Divisional Financial Executives", *Studies in Business Policy 101*, by C.G. Baumes, National Industrial Conference Board.

Ortman, R.F. (1975), "The Effects on Investment Analysis of Alternative Reporting Procedures for Diversified Firms", *The Accounting Review*, April, pp. 298–304.

Ouchi, W.G. (1979), "A Conceptual Framework for the Design of Organizational Control Mechanisms", *Management Science*, 25, September, pp. 833–48.

Ouchi, W.G. (1980), "Markets, Bureaucracies, and Clans", *Administrative Science Quarterly*, 25 March, pp. 129–41.

Parker, L.D. (1979), "Divisional Performance Measurement: Beyond an Exclusive Profit Test", *Accounting and Business Research*, No. 36, pp. 309–19.

Pike, R.H. (1983), "A Major Survey of the Investment Practices in Large Companies", *Institute of Cost and Management Accountants Occasional Paper*.

Ruefli, T.W. (1971a), "A Generalized Goal Decomposition Model", *Management Science*, April, pp. B/505–17.

Ruefli, T.W. (1971b), "Behavioural Externalities in Decentralized Organizations", *Management Science*, June, pp. B/649–57.

Scapens, R.W. (1979), "Profit Measurement in Divisionalised Companies", *Journal of Business Finance and Accounting*, Autumn, pp. 281–305.

Scapens, R.W. and Sale, J.T. (1981), "Performance Measurement and Formal Capital Expenditure Controls in Divisionalised Companies", *Journal of Business Finance and Accounting*, Autumn, pp. 389–419.

Scapens, R.W., Sale, J.T. and Tikkas, P.A. (1982), *Financial Control of Divisional Capital Investment*, ICMA Occasional Papers Series.

Scapens, R.W. and Sale, J.T. (1985), "An International Study of Accounting Practices in Divisionalised Companies and Their Association with Organisational Variables", *The Accounting Review*, LX (2), April, pp. 231–47.

Schall, L.D., Sundem, G.L. and Geijsbeek, W.R. (1978), "Survey and Analysis of Capital Budgeting Methods", *Journal of Finance*, 33, pp. 281–7.

Sharpe, W.F. (1964), "Capital Asset Prices: A Theory of Market Equilibrium Under Conditions of Risk", *Journal of Finance*, September.

Shillinglaw, G. (1957), "Guides to Internal Profit Measurement", *Harvard Business Review*, March–April, pp. 82–94.

Shillinglaw, G. (1961), "Problems in Divisional Profit Measurement", *NA(C)A Bulletin*, March, p. 33.

Shwayder, K. (1970), "A Proposed Modification to Residual Income – Interest Adjusted Income", *The Accounting Review*, April, pp. 299–307.

Simon, H. (1954), *Centralization and Decentralization in Organizing the Controller's Department*, Graduate School of Industrial Administration, Carnegie Institute of Technology.

Sloan, A.P. (1963), *My Years with General Motors*, Harmondsworth: Penguin Books.

Solomons, D. (1965), *Divisional Performance: Measurement and Control*, Financial Executives Research Foundation.

Spicer, B.H. and Ballew, V. (1983), "Management Accounting Systems and the Economics of Internal Organization", *Accounting, Organizations and Society*, 8 (1), pp. 73–96.

Thompson, J.D. (1967), *Organizations in Action*, McGraw-Hill.

Tiessen, P. and Waterhouse, J.H. (1983), "Towards a Descriptive Theory of Management Accounting", *Accounting, Organisations and Society*, pp. 251–68.

Tomkins, C. (1973), *Financial Planning in Divisionalised Companies*, London: Haymarket Publishing.

Tomkins, C. (1975), "Another Look at Residual Income", *Journal of Business Finance and Accounting*, 2 (1), Spring, pp. 39–53.

Williamson, O.E. (1970), *Corporate Control and Business Behavior*, Engle-wood Cliffs, NJ: Prentice-Hall.

Williamson, O.E. (1975), *Markets and Hierarchies: Analysis and Antitrust Implications*, New York: Free Press.

Williamson, O.E. (1981), "The Modern Corporation: Origins, Evolution, Attributes", *Journal of Economic Literature*, XIX, December, pp. 1537–68.

Williamson, O.E. and Bhargava, N. (1972), "Assessing and Classifying the Internal Structure and Control Apparatus of the Modern Corpor-ation", in K. Cowling (ed.), *Market Structure and Corporate Behaviour: Theory and Empirical Analysis of the Firm*, London: Gray-Mills Publishing.

Vancil, R.F. (1979), *Decentralization: Ambiguity by Design*, Irwin.

Vangermeersch, R. (1986), *The Contributions of Alexander Hamilton Church to Accounting and Management*, New York, Garland Publishing.

Vatter, W.J. (1959), "Does the Rate of Return Measure Business Efficiency?", *National Association of Accountants*, January.

Zimmerman, J.L. (1979), "The Costs and Benefits of Cost Allocation", *The Accounting Review*, July, pp. 504–21.

Index